Gangsters, Harlo
Down and Out at the Hotel Clifton

Edited by Theron Moore

road/house – Saint Vitus Press

Gangsters, Harlots and Thieves:
Down and Out at the Hotel Clifton

Editor: Theron Moore

Contact: stvitusfan@aol.com

Road/House – Saint Vitus Press

Printing History: First Edition, June 2011

The photo of the Hotel Clifton on the cover is property of the Stephenson County Historical Society and is reprinted herein with their express permission. It has been cropped and formatted by the author for artistic reasons pertaining to this book.

All poetry and prose in this book are property of the Moore family and cannot be reprinted without express written permission by the family.

All historical information regarding the Hotel Clifton was provided by Edward F. Finch, D.A., Executive Director of the Stephenson County Historical Society & Museum. The help I received from him and his staff during the writing of this book was invaluable. Thank you.

Commentary throughout this book is provided by Theron Moore, Jason Moore and Nancy Weir.

Three excerpts from a 2006 interview conducted with Todd Moore by Neil Wilgus appear in Chapters one, three and seven.

An excerpt from a 2006 interview conducted with Todd Moore by Anita L. Wynn appears in Chapter seven.

TABLE OF CONTENTS

DEDICATIONS

First and foremost, to my father, Todd Moore, who passed away March 12th 2010 at age 72.   He was a good husband, dad and one amazing writer. We all miss him a lot. He leaves behind a legacy and body of work that has taken on a life of its own. This book features his poetry and essays.

…are sent out to my mom, my brother and my wife Jeanette, who has been my rock and staunchest supporter during the writing of this book: 9-12-25.

…are also sent out to the entire Moore family, especially my Aunt Nancy and Uncle Wayne. Many thanks to Aunt Nancy for the help she gave me regarding the many family questions I had that I asked her during the writing of this book.

INTRODUCTION

I. TODD MOORE: LIKE A BEAUTIFUL NIGHTMARE

The drummer Roy Haynes said that playing with John Coltrane was *"like a beautiful nightmare."* Todd Moore's work might be described as *"like a beautiful nightmare."*

One of the co-founders of the **Outlaw Poetry Movement**, Todd Moore defined the literary outlaw. What is the outlaw poetry movement? What is Todd Moore all about? Todd Moore was a true revolutionary and his revolution was the outlaw revolution which is about an extreme individuality, an extreme viscerality, and an extreme velocity.

The outlaw appears when everything is stale, everything is boring, and everything is stagnating. The outlaw is about blood, intensity, and passion. Todd Moore dared to ask, *"Where is the blood, the meat, the raw guts of writing?"* Todd Moore dared to take poetry in a new direction. He revolutionized the short poem, yielding the poem with a punch, described as **"Poetry Noir"** or **"Killer Zen"**, which has influenced generations of poets.

He revolutionized the long poem with his classic work, *Dillinger*, volume after volume based on the archetype of bank robber, John Dillinger. And he revolutionized the essay, or autobiographical prose, through his poetry-essays, which often dealt with the theme of the outlaw, and which gave a glimpse of his own life.

He further revolutionized the poetic line, condensing the line in his later volumes of *Dillinger*, to reduce language to line breaks of short phrases and even syllables. He broke poetry down to its nuclear essence, the syllable. And he wrote with a velocity that would challenge a John Coltrane solo. He would catch a wave of intensity and go, go, go. While his later line of poetry would be slim, the work itself would be expansive. The combination is irresistible.

And if Todd Moore revolutionized writing in America, he also revolutionized thought. The obsessiveness which he brought to writing he brought to life itself. He wrote and wrote and wrote. Then he rested. And while resting, his ideas continued in his dreams. Even poetry readings were not just places to read poems, they were places to write poems.

And if he was not writing poems, he was writing essays, expressing his ideas about subjects related to his outlaw philosophy. He was a walking, talking ball of fire, carrying his own revolutionary energy.

To be an outlaw is to be one who creates one's own laws, one's own style, one's own thought. To be an outlaw is to be one who is out on the side, one who is marginal, one who is alone in the margins.

Todd Moore was the lone individual who created his own path, his own way, his own journey. Todd Moore and I co-founded the outlaw movement in poetry. We discussed outlaw poetry and outlaw thought in the early 1980's, around the time Todd published a volume of mine called *Outlaw Blues*.

We continued the outlaw dialogue through the years and many of the outlaw poems, ideas, and essays appeared in a publication begun in 2001 and edited by Todd and his son Theron, *St. Vitus Press and Poetry Review* (www.saintvituspress.com).

In 2004, Todd and I began emailing each other and identifying what we meant by "outlaw" and "the outlaw movement." These ideas are readily defined in essays and interviews by Todd Moore and me and we identified 2004 as the official year for the founding of the outlaw movement.

-- Tony Moffeit

II. HE WAS MY FATHER

The way

i write
is strictly
fuck you
no cap
ital letters
no punc
tuation
the words
jammed together
or all
smashed
up like brok
ken glass
crushed
pop cans
& used
condoms
the ameri
can sen
tence is
either a
stutter
or a
scream
& i'm
waiting
to watch
it explode

That poem is precisely my father's voice in both his writing and real life as well – straight shooter, to the point, no frills. That was dad. I can honestly say that when it came to the craft of writing, poetry specifically, he took it all very, very seriously. If you really want to know who my father was, here's a title from a poem he wrote back in the 80's: *"I like a poem hard like a bullet."*

That very quote defined him as a writer. That's how he saw himself and others saw him as well. He was part Johnny Cash, part Sam Peckinpah and part Lemmy from Motorhead.

My father was an outlaw poet. *It* created my father as much as my father co-created the genre itself. This style of writing was a natural direction / progression for him. When you sit down and read this book, you'll see and understand how easily the outlaw portion of his personality was developed and how it found its way into my father's writing, how it came out when he put pen to paper and how and why he would embrace it the way he did as a writer.

As a kid my dad was a self confessed juvenile delinquent; *"i was a street thief, a dime store bandit. Whatever wasn't nailed down was automatically mine."* He never shied away from admitting that when asked. He and his sister, my Aunt Nancy, used to steal whatever they thought they could sell to the local scrap yard – iron, paper, etc.

"I pretty much lived on, off, and from the street when I was a kid and I stole lots of shit and the things I loved to steal most were wanted posters right off the post office walls. They were always stapled to a bulletin board near the front door so I had to time the act of ripping one off just right so that I wouldn't be seen by anyone entering or leaving the building. Usually, the clerks were so busy weighing packages they didn't realize what was going on."
– Todd Moore

In fact, my father often told me that he'd steal copper tubing from the local railroad yard and then sell it back to them later. He also mentioned a jewelry store that he and friends would break into via the roof. He wouldn't tell me what they stole though, just that they did it on numerous occasions.

"I hate to say your father and I stole things as kids because that's not a good thing to admit, but we did. That was back when we were in elementary and junior high, right around that timeframe. A lot of the stuff we'd do would be taking whatever we could find, whether it

was ours or someone else's property, to the scrap yard and sell it. We'd take the money and head to the show and watch movies all day.

I remember one time we got in trouble for selling this huge iron wheel we found it in an alley behind the Clifton, figured no one would miss it. Made some good money down at the scrap yard.

Whoever it was, they suspected it might've been stolen and the guy from the scrap yard called dad. We had been down there selling stuff enough times that they knew who we were. They threatened to call the police on us if we didn't return the cash. Dad was so mad at us, I mean, he was hot."
-- Nancy Weir

This book is an important snapshot of my father's life growing up at the Hotel Clifton as a kid because for the first time we see what the circumstances were that piqued his interest in wanting to be a writer and for this reason alone I wanted that documented using his own voice, through his own poetry and essays.

My father's life as a small press writer is quite well known. Up until now, this chapter of his life hasn't been told to this extent, with this much detail. Now it has.

I wrote this book because I wanted to honor my father and his writing legacy, but I also did it as a way of dealing with his death which is still difficult for me at times, over a year later.

I wish I could give credit to all of the publications where these poems and essays might have previously appeared, but I can't. He was published extensively over the last 40 years in hundreds of publications, yet never kept accurate records of such things, so to those folks who might've previously published any of this material, my apologies to you, it wasn't an intentional omission, I just didn't have any available information to go on.

Enjoy, Thank you!
-- Theron Moore

Essays and Poetry
By Todd Moore

Edited by Theron Moore

Chapter 1

The Hotel Clifton & Café

Neil Wilgus: Let's begin with your life so far. You've written that you had one hell of a struggle growing up. What was it like and how has it influenced your writing?

Todd Moore: I could probably write a memoir or a novel on this question and have often considered it. But most of that life I covered one way or another in the poetry. But here is an abbreviated version. My father was strictly blue collar. Railroad man, then nineteen years on the fire department until they canned him for alcoholism. What he really wanted to be was a writer and was damned good at telling stories but not writing them.

Between drinking and writing, he went down for the count sometime around 1949 when I was twelve years old. Hit the skids and came to a screeching halt in a dive called the Clifton Hotel, a joint that catered to railroad men, drifters, con artists, sociopaths, hookers, and assorted outlaws. On the way to this psychological train wreck, we lost everything. Furniture, most of our personal effects, you name it. Sold at auction to pay off the bills.

It was like being shipwrecked in the middle of a cornfield. My father spent the next couple of years bartending, sweeping out honkytonks, cadging for drinks. And, I grew up one step away from living on the street. The flat we lived in was two rooms connected with a dark hallway, a bare bulb, and a bare bones toilet next to what passed for a kitchen. No shower, no bath tub.

Six of us slept on one room, living room in the day time, bedroom at night. A former tenant had punched a giant sized hole in the wall above my roll away bed exposing the studs. At night the rats used to go back and forth behind that wood. Sometimes I imagined them stopping to watch me. So, I grew up outlaw and I grew up fast.

Excerpt from the essay
The Dark Side of America

... I could hear the rat in the hole in the wall above my old rickety fold up bed.

I could hear the way his little claws were going over rotten wood and I would lie perfectly still and think he's staring at me, I can feel his eyes going all over me. I never got him but I wanted to, I wanted to kill that rat more than anything else but when that hole got plugged up I know he went somewhere else in the hotel's walls.

I just know that he escaped and was in there waiting and you wouldn't be able to see him even if you could somehow crawl into the space of that wall, maybe all you would be able to see were his eyes. The thought of his eyes went straight through me. I wanted to get him in the eyes because I knew that his soul wasn't too far away...

sleeping w/rats

at the clifton
hotel the
hole in the
wall above
the cot where
i slept had
a little
cracked
board nailed
over it
but that
wasn't enough
to keep them
from prowling
past me
in the dark
sometimes
they were
nothing more
than a scraping
of claws or
a quick
dark blur
other times
they sat above
me poised
in a nest of
dust & rotting
wood & i
listened to
those rat teeth
clicking
while they ate

My father and his family had moved into The Clifton Hotel circa 1947. My dad had two brothers and one sister – Gary, Neil and Nancy. By this time, the place was a wreck. The building and facilities had fallen into great disrepair and whatever former elegance it once had years and years before was now replaced with a skid row look and feel.

The hotel's occupants were a mix of thugs, hookers, thieves and professional drunks. As my Aunt Nancy said, it became "...a place for people to stay who were down on their luck."

To give you an idea of how seedy the joint was, my father recounted a story to me about going back to Freeport several years ago for a high school reunion and was approached by a lady, then a young girl, he used to know. My Aunt Nancy confirmed this story to me as well.

My father said, "...she came up to me, introduced herself and we spoke. She told me that she used to have a crush on me when we were kids but was too frightened to want to approach me, let alone date me, because of where I lived. She was scared to walk by the Clifton."

In 1961 my father moved out and attended Northern Illinois University on a teaching scholarship. That same year Earl Moore, my dad's father, passed away. He was sober when he died.

Using the insurance money, the rest of his family moved a few blocks away into a clean apartment where my grandmother lived for the rest of her life. My aunt Nancy still lives in Freeport. My uncle Gary lives in neighboring Cherry Valley. In 1965 the Clifton was sold, razed and replaced with a car dealership. The Freeport Public Library now resides on that very property.
-- **Theron Moore**

"The Clifton was filthy and stunk bad, I mean, there was a café on the ground floor and you could smell it everywhere. Dad told me never to eat there. He said he'd see cockroaches everywhere, even in the kitchen, and the cooks would kill them and cook them up with whatever they were cooking on the grill at the time, they didn't care.

We were constantly killing cockroaches and those horrible silver fish. I remember when we finally moved out of the Clifton into the apartment down the street, Ma told us to pack up everything we had except the bugs, they could stay. I can remember dad spraying in that apartment of ours in the Clifton killing all these bugs and then a few days later they were back in full force. And the hallways smelled like garbage from that café on the ground level.

Like I said before, the Clifton was full of people who were, well, down on their luck at the time and the Clifton wasn't the only hotel like this in Freeport, there was maybe one or two others. Lots of bad people there.

And we heard yelling and shouting all the time, people getting into fights, arguing. We had a suicide there too. Guy put a rope around his neck and jumped out of one of the windows. I saw it."

-- Nancy Weir

i saw the

rope milo used
to hang him
self w/ the
night clerk
had it coiled
on top of
the check in
desk did he
leave a note
i asked who
was he going
to write it to
the night clerk
sd taking a
hit off what
ever it was he
kept in the
thermos then
he leaned a
cross the rope
i kept the ten
he had in
his hat he
flashed me a
look then
shoved old
milo's jack
knife across
the counter i
smiled & sd
i won't tell

The locals, The Gunsels, The Shitheads, The bugs

Sweating now just the same way as I was sweating then. At the old hotel. Always in a sweat then. A fevered sweat and a frenzy. A frenzy that danced right at the ends of my fingertips and hair. A frenzy and a sweat and a fury to reach into that black place where all the best stories come from. To reach into that black place and haul out the best of all possible stories.

But, that had to wait until later because the hotel itself intruded on everything. That rotting hulk of an old hotel with its yellow brick façade and it's rotting wood interiors. I swear to god I could've been led blindfolded into the lobby and the odor would've given it away.

It was equal parts cheap wine, phlegm, urine, mixed generously with the stench of unwashed bodies, greasy food and coffee coming from the café, with just a touch of shit striped drawers, a dash of armpit, and if cockroaches give off a smell then lots and lots of flattened cockroaches under the worn out carpet.

And when a resident hooker walked by everything went to Moonlight and Roses Vat Number 5 from Woolworths. And, if I listened closely I could hear that nylon on nylon on vagina switch past. My father, sitting behind the registration desk sporting a green eyeshade and a cigarette, would stick his nose in the air and say something like, "*Are the fish biting today or what?*"

Outside, the long neon sign that was always shorting out read "**HOTEL CLIFTON.**" The neon, of course, was faint red. Not so deep as blood. More like faded lipstick. And, in the summer the doorway was usually jammed up with bugs trying to get into or out of the joint.

My old man used to keep a pint of Calvert under the counter. "*For the cough,*" he liked to say. He did have one hell of a cough, but that liquor worked on more than his cough. He'd tip that whiskey bottle neck, give me a wink, and take a nice long pull. Then he'd say, "*I gotta spell myself or this shit won't last the night.*"

Suddenly, some wise guy railroader would stroll by and say something like, "*Pal, maybe you won't last the night.*" My old man couldn't pass that one up. He'd flip a coin, call heads, snap his fingers and say, "*I might be shy a drop or two, but death, that old motherfucker ain't getting my ass tonight.*"

Finished with that little repartee, my old man would motion me over and say, "*Pack a smoke, kid, and some juicy fruit gum. Gotta get that shit taste outta my mouth,*" and he'd slap a dollar bill into my palm.

Then he'd wave me around the counter and I'd go back to where he was and he'd lean real close and say real low, *"Kid, this is just Hollywood for the locals, the gunsels, and the shitheads. You know me. You know who I am."*

Then, I'd say, *"How's the book coming along?"* and he'd say, *"Kid, writing a book is a cocksucker. Don't let anyone tell you different. But I got it. Yeah, fucken a, I got it all right here,"* he said pointing at his head, *"and here,"* pointing to his heart. *"One a these days, kid, one a these days my ship is gonna come in for sure."*

Once, when I came back with a ham sandwich from the Rainbow Grill, made just the way my old man liked it, with horseradish, mustard, sliced onions and tomatoes, I saw a guy in a black coat and no tie standing at the counter. And he and my old man were really getting into it.

When he saw me, he stopped in mid sentence and said, *"This your kid?"*

"Depends," my old man said, unwrapping the sandwich.

"That's a hellish stack a meat. You ain't gonna eat that thing are you? He really your kid?"

"What's your point?"

"Do I have to have a point?" Turning to me, the guy said, *"Your old man's a good one, alright."*

Before I could say anything, my old man pulled the wrapped half of a baseball bat out from under the counter. The guy saw it and eased his coat back to uncover a pistol butt. Then, he said, *"Waddya wanna bet I can hit a homerun with this before you can hit a homerun with that."* Pretty soon, the baseball bat went away and my old man just stood there while the guy with the gun in his belt was tapping his thumb against its grip.

Finally, the guy said, *"You can't keep a guy like Frankie waiting for his money. You oughta know that."*

"I'll settle up at the end of the month."

"Is that what you want me to tell Frankie?"

"Yeah, that's what I want you to tell Frankie."

"Absolutely and for sure." My father's face looked like a big red meat balloon with sweat all over it.

"*Hey, kid,*" the guy said, waving me over. "*Here's a buck for whatever you want. Candy, pop, the movies.*" Then, to my father he said, "*Frankie likes kids.*" He made a point of letting the pistol butt show as he walked away.

My old man motioned me over and said, "*I got an idea for the book, but before I can tell you about it, I got a shot a Calvert that needs a cup a joe.*"

sitting at the counter

in the clifton café
watching blind jesse
wilson trying to
eat his vegetable
soup w/one hand &
hold onto his beaten
up martin w/the
other & all of a
sudden he opened
his mouth for more
soup & a blow
fly buzzed in & the
minute he tried to
spit it out his uppers
went flying across
the wood that's
when he glanced at
me w/dead eyes &
sd whoevers got my
teeth i ain't got any
reward money
that's ok i sd
handing his teeth
back hows abt
when yr finished
we go outside
& you sing me a
little of yr death
song blues

sitting over

coffee in the
clifton café
when waco
shoved the
oblong pack
age across
the table he
grinned &
sd open it
when i
ripped
the butcher
paper
the first
thing i saw
was the
brown lea
ther grip
of a black
jack merry
xmas he sd
rubbing the
scar on his
cheek i used
it on milo
the bones in
his nose
snapped like
sticks in a
sack

reno took a

sip of the coffee
i got him & sd
the clifton's the
kinda joint where
you can hole up
& get lost he
was playing a
round w/a 45
auto slapping the
clip in then re
leasing it you
like guns he
asked handing
it over yeah i sd
it looks like some
thing bogart wd
carry reno smiled
his crooked smile
sat way back in
side his shadow
& sd wadda you
like about it i
kept my finger
off the trigger
like he told me
playing w/it i
sd aiming at my
self in the mir
ror a laugh came
out of the sha
dow & reno sd
jesus kid yr play
ing w/death

malone sat

across from me
at a table
in the clifton
café sd
how's yr old
man & before
i cd answer
stopped a
waitress &
sd gimme a
refill of that
paint you call
coffee then
glancing back
at me sd
yr old man
& i go way
back when the
waitress left
he passed a
38 special
under the
table sd
tell him
i'm flat
busted &
all out of
dreams but
he's welcome
to this it's
part of the
story & part
of the blood

"I can remember dad telling me a story about the time he was hanging out with his father in the back of the Clifton Hotel next to a burn barrel. He had a bottle in one hand and the novel he had written in the other.

He was drunk, pissed off, why I can't remember, but, it had something to do with his book.

Each time he took a drink he'd tear a page out and throw it into the fire. Dad, he was just a young kid at the time, just stood there and watched. It had an impact on him, something he never forgot about. I think it might've been a turning point for him."
-- Jason Moore

Stories, Ashes, and Fire

There used to be a fire barrel out behind the Clifton Hotel. And, everything got burned up in it. Newspapers, magazines, letters with blood on them letters about nothing but blood, old photographs, bills both paid and unpaid, the cries of the anguished written directly on skin peeled away from the bone. Entire histories of human suffering went into the fire.

Along with outlines for stories I couldn't write, hundreds maybe thousands of poems that died before they were born, names of all the aliases of the drifters who floated in and out of that hotel, gambling IOU's, death threats, secret account books, pages from both Genesis and The Book of Revelations the kid who threw them in said *"Revelations burned the best."*

The names of the lost, the names of the dead. Garbage. Everything that could be incinerated was torched in that barrel.

I was standing there watching the fire crawl up the side of an old shoebox when Jerry ran up and dropped some red sticks into the flames. Then he ran off about twenty feet before he turned and yelled, *"Get the fuck out of there!"*

I said, *"What were those red sticks?"*

He said, *"You stupid bastard. Those weren't red sticks. They were twelve gauge shotgun shells."*

I ducked behind a wall just as something blew a hole in the side of the fire barrel and all kinds of shit flew out. I said, *"Jesus Christ, Jerry, are you trying to kill me?"*

He danced like a chicken going *bicaw-bicaw* with his big arms going up and down when the second and third shells went off, some of the pellets peppering the side of the hotel. *"Goddamn!"* he yelled. *"Did you see that?? I love it when everything blows!"*

He danced like a chicken going *bicaw-bicaw* with his big arms going up and down when the second and third shells went off, some of the pellets peppering the side of the hotel. *"Goddamn!"* he yelled. *"Did you see that?? I love it when everything blows!"*

I watched a guy burn a wanted poster with his picture on it in the fire barrel. I was able to read the name under his photo.

I said, *"Is your name really Jack North?"*

He looked at me, took a switchblade out of his pocket, clicked it open, ran the blade up and down his bare arm like he was sharpening the steel on his skin and said, *"No, from now on its Jack West."*

Sometimes the old woman who owned the hotel would come out. She reminded me of a cinder wearing a soiled white dress. She never talked very much. Somebody once told me that she was really into heroin and maybe my old man was her connection, or at the very least her connection's connection. She was also a drunk.

Once she asked me if I was the one who liked to start fires. I said no. I could have told her it was Dickie Boy Johnson who lived down the street but instead I just kept quiet.

I could tell by the way she looked she didn't believe me. She said if I burned the hotel down I wouldn't have anywhere to live. Did I really want that? I thought about telling her that living in the hotel was like living nowhere, nowhere at all. But I kept my mouth shut because my old man was the night clerk but I gave her a look.

She said *"You know you are an outlaw, a fucking little firebug outlaw. "*

I said, *"You better watch out. You're standing too close to the fire."*

She put her right hand directly over the flames for a few quick seconds, then took it away and said, *"You can never be too close to a fire like this."*

She reached into her purse for a Kleenex. I thought she was going for the little 25 auto she was supposed to be carrying and I stepped back. She gave me a bone smile and floated off in the smoke.

Lonny J liked to tell about the switchman who murdered a hooker, cut her to pieces, and burned them up in the fire barrel. Lonny said he wasn't living in the hotel at the time but would come by nights and toss big chunks of meat into the fire.

I couldn't tell by looking at Lonny's face if he was telling the truth or just bullshitting me because he always walked around with a stupid smirk on his face. But, when I called him on it, he would start to bite his arm and make the blood come. Once he even flicked some of his blood on me.

Sometimes I would see the switchman walking down the street and I would start looking at him. He had a funny shaped face. It was long and angular and almost bent in places. One day he stopped me and said *"If you keep staring at me that way I am going to have to do something. And, you won't like it."*

My old man once told me that he had cold cocked a guy with a ball peen hammer and it left a soft spot in the back of the guy's skull. The switchman was standing up close when he said it and I had my hand in my pocket on my switchblade knife. I didn't know if I could cut anyone but I wasn't going to let him do something either.

Once in the winter while I was burning some old papers just to watch the fire go, my old man came out of the hotel and walked over. He was holding a pint of Jim Beam which had maybe one or two swallows left in it.

He said, *"Did you know that death is in there?"*

I said, *"No, I didn't. How can you tell?"*

He took a hit of Beam and said, *"Death smells like old rags burning. Old rags all covered with blood. He's in there all right. I can smell him the way I can smell a hooker from a block away."*

Then he touched me on the shoulder and said, *"If death came to the door looking for me, would you ever let him in?"*

I swallowed hard and said, I never heard of death doing anything like that. *"But, he does,"* my old man said. *"He does it every single day. And, when he isn't knocking on doors, he's waiting in there."*

He used his whiskey hand to point at the fire barrel. He waited a few seconds and said again, *"Would you ever let him in?"* I swallowed hard again and said, *"No."*

"And, if he does get in. Death is a sneaky motherfucker." My old man was standing so close to me that some of his whiskey spit was hitting me in the face. *"What if he gets in?"*

"Why, then, I'll take a butcher knife to his eyes."

A smile cracked my old man's face in two and he said, "*Christ, that's one to remember. Even if this is the last day of my life, that's one to remember.*"

The thing that I noticed about Smitty was he was holding a bottle of whiskey except that it wasn't filled with whiskey. It was filled with gasoline and Smitty had corked it with a ripped shirt tail for a rag but it wasn't lit yet and he was standing close to the fire barrel and all kinds of flames were pouring out.

Smitty glanced over at me and said, "*You dare me?*"

I waited a couple of seconds and said, "*Why don't we blow it up down at the river.*"

He said, "*I wanna feel the fire get on me, I wanna feel the fire get all over me.*"

"*You wanna die?*" I asked.

"*I just wanna feel the fire get on me. Lets take it down to the river and blow up some hobo shack.*"

Smitty said, "*Can we shoot guns?*"

I smiled and said, "*Sure, let's go shoot guns.* "

The second Smitty gave me the Molotov cocktail and I stepped back, some sparks went up and missed us by inches.

My old man's novel went into that fire barrel. And, maybe all of my poetry comes out of it. I remember burning a short story I wrote after reading Hemingway's "*The Killers.*"

I stood close and watched the manuscript slide in. I remember burning a long poem I wrote after reading Whitman's "*Song of Myself.*" I remember burning a novel I wrote after reading Jack London's Call Of The Wild.

My old man was standing in a black rain of scorched paper when he burned the only story he ever knew in that goddam barrel. Some of those ashes got caught in my clothes. And, no matter how hard I tried to shake them out, I couldn't get them all.

Some of them are still in there, even now. They heat me with their unbearable, their unforgiving darkness.

burning

houses my
old man
sd licking
a drop
of whiskey
off the
back of
his hand
you can't
beat them
for drama
the way
flaming
timbers fall
across a
sofa or a
kitchen
sink clouds
of sparks
shooting
out the door
some nights
i sleep in
fire i always
walk in
smoke

Excerpt from the essay
The Nightmare of Poetry is War

      I never wrote anything at the Clifton Hotel that was worth a shit. I think I might have been able to. Maybe. I had all of that darkness packed inside me. But it was mostly the smell. The rotting carpet, the shitty furniture, the gone wood, the whiskey and body odor stench, the whole visceral gut wrenching vomit reek of the place. It was as real, as palpable as the people who lived there. Now, when I write about that place I practically have to reinvent it brick by brick.

fuller went

down on his
knees on
the first floor
landing &
puked a
red stream
down the
hotel stairs
the shit
went up
in a ragged
arc &
came down
hard
splattering
every step
except the
last one
then he did
the dry
heaves
3 times
wiped his
face on
his sleeve
& sd i
can still
taste the
chili
that rita
smeared on
her cunt

sitting

in the clif
ton café w/
my old
man who
was rock
ing back
& forth
in his chair
trying to
decide
if he was
going to
drink the
black cof
fee or take
another
hit from
the bottle
of rye
stuck be
tween his
legs he
glanced
at me
sd
i'm still
gonna
write that
railroad
novel
he made
his eyes
into a pair
of black
slits
& a wes
tern too
i got one

more in
me
then he
sd fuck
& sprayed
some whis
key spit
in my
direction
he put his
head back
hawked
up some
phlegm
& let
it spill out
of his
mouth
& in
to the
coffee
then
he leaned
forward
sd
i wish
i had a
little
38 he came
close &
i cd feel
the heat
radiating
off his face
what do
you need
a 38 for
i asked
he stared
at me a

few seconds
sd
research
when you
put guns
in the
story you
shd know
how they
work
something
inside
him was
shaking
& he
cdn't make
it stop
he reached
into his
coat poc
ket brought
out a few
ones &
threw them
at me
sd
go to
the movies
christ
when you
live like
this it's
the only
dream
that you
got

Devouring the Shadow

I live somewhere between the click of a pistol hammer and a Molotov cocktail with a rag fuse burning. I write somewhere between the light from a house fire and the night reflected off a shotgun barrel. I dream somewhere between the illuminated sweat piling off Dillinger's face and a stuttered machine gun flash in the noon of my darkness.

It's 1947. I'm watching a railroad cop blackjack a drifter. First, he dragged the guy out of a freight car by the collar and threw him across the tracks. Next, he gave the guy a hard kick to the face.

The blow had a dull meaty sound that resonated between boxcars parked on the siding. Last, he pulled out a flat blackjack and began to give him quick roundhouse shots to the side of the head. And, this wasn't a sloppy beating. It was methodical, no missed swings.

And, when it was over he dragged the drifter over to the steep embankment and threw him down into the brush. He looked like the gamblers I knew who never showed any emotion.

Then the cop glanced over to where I was standing.

"What's your name kid?" His voice didn't fit what he had just done. It was soft, not high pitched, but almost gentle. *"Kids like you could die in places like this."* He was walking toward me and I should've run away but somehow my feet were rooted to the cinders where I stood.

When he got close he said, *"You're Earl's kid, aincha?"*

"Yeah" I said.

"I thought I seen you around here. I won't tell your old man. See, we go back. The twenties. We used to do a little you know bootlegging on the side."

He took a deep breath, glanced over at the bushes where he'd thrown the drifter and said, *"Times change."* Then he took a Hershey bar out of his coat, tore off the wrapper, and gave me half.

After I finished the candy bar, he reached inside his coat and straightened his shoulder holster. Then he took a flask out of his pocket and did a hit of what I think was whiskey.

He said, *"You get home you tell your old man Tracy says hello. You got that?"*

"Yeah," I replied.

What Billy Ray used to do was stand on street corners with his grandmother in the wheelbarrow. A different one every day. She would hold a sign that read, *"I am an old Christian woman and have no money. Could you please spare me some change?"*

She had an old beaten up Stetson hat sitting upside down in her lap and people would go by feeling sorry for her and before long the hat would begin to fill up with nickels, dimes, quarters, even one dollar bills.

After she thought they'd collected enough she'd say, "*It's time to go to Larry's.*"

Larry's was a diner down on Main Street that had the greasiest fries in town.

Billy Ray's grandmother never liked to talk much. She'd say things like, "*Ain't it a fine day or I think the weather's gonna turn cold, I can feel the black wind in my bones.*"

Sometimes she'd say, "*It looks like it's gonna be dark today. I don't like it when it gets dark in the daytime.*"

Billy Ray and his grandmother lived on the second floor of the Clifton Hotel.

The first time I met her I wondered how she could ever make it up and down those steps, but when I saw her race up the steps two at a time, I realized that there was more to the grandmother than I might ever know.

Billy Ray never liked it when she did that. He'd say," *It's gonna be bad for business.*" All she did was put her finger to her lips to hush him up and it never failed to work.

Billy Ray and his grandmother only stayed at the hotel just that spring and summer. Then they caught a bus out of town. It didn't surprise me that they didn't take the wheelbarrow along. It was probably borrowed or stolen anyway.

The day before they left, I said to the grandmother, "*Where is your husband?*"

Billy Ray said, "*Don't tell him anything.* "

The grandmother gave Billy Ray a look and said, "*Nonsense. Gimme a dollar and I'll tell you all about it.*"

I took a dollar out of my wallet and the grandmother did a funny little dance, stuffed it down her dress and said, "*He was a good for nothing. Never did anything that amounted to a lick so I shot him.*"

I tried not to act surprised.

"*Does Billy Ray miss his father?*" I asked.

"*Heavens, that man wasn't his father, and Billy Ray isn't my grandson, he's my man, just a little small for his age but it works for the good of the business.*"

jerry's old man

was in love
w/agnes the
one legged
hooker who lived
in the hotel
& what jerry &
i liked to do
was fuck a
round outside
the hotel room
laughing
making noise til
his old man paid
us to go to the
movies after
he slapped the
money into
jerry's hand he'd
say yr just a
coupla con
artists is all
doncha have any
respect for a
man who needs
to get laid
as soon as we
left jerry wd say
waddya think
she's got in that
stump & that
wd make me
laugh & i'd say
firecrackers
hershey bars &
a skanky taste
of bone

Chapter 2

My Old Man was a Tough Guy

the snap brim

stetson & the
dark gray
suit made my
old man
look like
philip marlowe
& the way
he stood
for that
kodak shot
it looks like
he's leaning
a little to
the side
like he's
drunk or
so filled w/
the raw
meat of
darkness he
can't stand
straight
this is the
man i wanted
to talk to
i wanted to
ask abt
his dreams
& his guns

Workin' for the "Big Fellow," Al Capone

Capone spent a lot of time in Freeport. I know that he owned several speakeasies and ran numbers as well.
-- **Nancy Weir**

"What dad told me was that our grandfather Earl did indeed work for Capone in Freeport. He was basically a small time bookie. He also told me that Earl once got busted by Capone's guys for a little bootlegging. They basically pulled him aside and "convinced" him that he needed to stop doing this since. He did what he was told, he stopped and that was that."
-- **Jason Moore**

"In regards to what my brother said above, my father talked about this quite a bit and my Aunt Nancy confirmed it as well. In fact, she told me that her father-in-law knew Capone also, just how much and to what extent, I don't really know.

She said that he didn't talk about it much because you just didn't do that kind of thing back then. You did what you were told, took what was given to you and kept your mouth shut about it.

My overall feeling is that if you were seen as a guy who was willing to do odd jobs and /or run errands and you could be trusted, you could probably find work with Capone and his crew, as long as someone could vouch for you so you could have that kind of "in."

It isn't quite known how old my grandfather Earl was when he met Capone although I do know that the timeframe in question would have to have been sometime between 1921 and 1928, this much is for sure."
-- **Theron Moore**

sitting

on the front
stoop of
the clifton w/
my old man
who has a
bottle of
beam be
tween his
feet on the
cement &
he's tell
ing me abt
the old
time leggers
the big
players out
of chica
go who
breezed
thru town
w/platinum
blondes &
machine guns
sez the time
i met ca
pone he
smiled so
wide it
looked like
a wound

Alcoholism

"When my father was sober, he was the kindest, funniest person you'd ever meet. Very charming, very down to earth, but when he was drinking, he changed. He'd disappear on drinking binges and could occasionally be very abusive, verbally, to our mother and in a lot of ways that's a lot worse than physical abuse. Words can hurt so much more."

*"Before we lived at the Clifton we were living over on Shawnee Street in a house next to this bar, **The Shawnee Tap**, and that's where dad's drinking really started. He was a bartender there, part time, while still working for the fire department. When he lost his job as a fireman, we had to move, I mean, we had no money, we were broke, we had no choice.*

So ma took all of us kids to Oregon to live with Uncle Bill and his wife, whose name I can't remember at the moment. That was in 1947. I was 5 years old, Todd was 10 years old and Gary was 8 years old.

We lived there for six months, went to school there too. In fact, Todd was held back a year because of this. I don't think they liked us living there a whole lot because as kids we were pretty active and pulled practical jokes around the house, sometimes on uncle Bill and I don't think he appreciated that too much. You know, they were older and we were just being young kids, you know?

All this time, dad was back in Freeport trying to find a job. He eventually found work as a night watchman over at Furst McNess and moved us into this rundown, horrible place called The Clifton Hotel where he also found work as a part time night clerk.

We had an apartment there. It was bad. It was an actual hotel that you could stay at for cheap but you could rent apartments in it as well. The people who lived there were down on their luck at the time and couldn't afford to live anywhere else. There were some good people there who just couldn't afford anything else but mainly a lot of drunks and people like that. Very skid row.

We were there from 1948 to 1960, up until dad died. I was 16 when he passed away, and by that time he had given up drinking, he was sober. I was a junior in high school at the time. Ma took the insurance money, bought a car and found a clean apartment that was just a few blocks down the street and we moved. Up until then we never owned a car."

-- **Nancy Weir**

Dreaming of my Old Man's Tooth

The day my old man pulled his own tooth with old pliers by the radiator with the paint chipping off, I tried to steal it. He had bled out on a ragged towel and had set the tooth on it. The thing was yellow, black in places.

The blood on the roots was already beginning to darken. He was drinking Jim Beam he said to cauterize the wound and after every shot he gagged and spit into a torn off square of bed sheet and what he was spitting out was red.

I wanted that tooth more than anything and I don't exactly know why except that it belonged to my old man and looked dark and forbidding and i really wanted to show it off to my friends.

I wanted to say, I stole this from my old man, maybe even make them think I was so tough I'd knocked it out of his mouth. I wanted to be the first kid maybe almost anywhere who could pull his old man's tooth out of his pants pocket and wave it around and make stories up about it.

I wanted that tooth and I wanted that blood and I think my old man sensed it, felt it in his bones, maybe even smelled my overpowering desire to have it and before I could make a move he scooped it off the bed, licked whatever blood was still on the roots, gagged into a ripped square of bed sheet and said, *"You can't have it."*

His jaw was a little swollen where the tooth had come out. His eyes were almost bugging out of his head when he said *"You got your own teeth. You can't have mine."* Then he took another healthy chug of Jim Beam and coughed red spit into the rag.

I don't know whatever happened to that old bloody tooth. I suspect he may have burned it because a few hours later I watched him stand at the old trash barrel out behind the hotel. He used a lighter to set the blood stained towel on fire. He held it out over the barrel until the flames had crawled halfway up the towel. Then he dropped it in and watched the fire consume it.

As an afterthought he reached into his shirt pocket, took out what I think was the tooth and dropped it into the smoke. For a few savage moments, light from the fire put long red slashes across his face. He looked like a man who was burning.

Later on, when I first started writing poetry, I would pretend that I had the tooth back, that my old man had kept the tooth instead of burning it up and that when he died he left me the tooth along with a broken jack knife and a pocket watch that never worked. I would pretend that before writing a poem I would take the tooth out.

In my fantasy, I kept the tooth wrapped up in an old handkerchief secured by a rubber band and when I wasn't writing I had the tooth hidden on the bookshelf behind a book of short stories by Ernest Hemingway called <u>Men Without Women</u>.

I especially like to have it behind this book because the bookmark was an old strip of miniature snapshots of men taken a hundred years ago. I used to pretend that these guys were desperadoes, maybe members of Butch Cassidy's *Hole In The Wall Gang* and that the tooth would be right at home behind this book that contained stories like *"The Undefeated," "The Killers,"* and *"Fifty Grand."*

And, when I was working on a poem, I'd take the book off the shelf, reach back and get hold of the handkerchief the tooth was wrapped in. Then, I would start the ritual of carefully undoing the rubber band and unwrapping the frayed handkerchief.

When I had the corners of the cloth spread out, I'd sit and stare at the tooth for awhile, just to let the sight of it work on me. Allow its magic to cover me with darkness.

Finally, I'd slowly reach out and pick it up. It was rough to the hand; the edges of the tooth were sharp and jagged. But that didn't matter because it was my good luck charm. Some guys carried old shell casings, rabbit's feet, lucky coins. In this, the best of all possible fantasies, i had my old man's tooth.

Sometimes in the fantasy, the lines of a poem would come to me while I was holding my old man's tooth. Whenever this happened i could feel the skin along my spine begin to tingle, almost as though the words all by themselves carried some kind of electrical charge. As soon as that happened I knew i had a poem. I knew it as much as I had ever known anything. And, in that fantasy the feeling never betrayed me.

I held onto that fantasy for as long as I could. And, then I realized that I could get poems without dreaming my old man's tooth into existence. I could get them just by driving down the highway, by throwing stones at the river, by waking up in the dark. I could almost get a poem by reaching into my pocket. The poems were always there just under the surface of what it was that I was dreaming.

So, I let the fantasy of my old man's tooth go into the river with all of my thrown away stones. One day along about sundown while standing on the bank of the Kishwaukee River i reached into my pocket and threw my old man's tooth out as far as I could.

I pretended I could see it arc high in the air and then dip toward the water. I imagined the splash and I imagined it going under the water, sinking to the bottom of one of the river's many holes.

I often wonder if Melville kept a whale's tooth near his desk, if Hemingway ever used a lion's tooth to conjure a story, if London carried a wolf's fang. The only thing I ever learned from conjuring my old man's tooth to call down a poem was that it was all in the dreaming. The trick was to believe in everything to make the words bleed out of the thousand wounds of darkness.

I still have Hemingway's <u>Men Without Women</u> with the miniature strip of desperado faces. Some things like Papa's story *"The Killers"* you just simply can't do without. Even though I don't read *"The Killers"* anymore, it feels good that the story is still there. As for my old man's tooth, one night I dreamt that I went back to the old hotel and put it back on the towel while my old man was gagging up blood.

Excerpt from the essay
Going to meet the Outlaw

I pretty much lived on, off, and from the street when I was a kid and I stole lots of shit and the things I loved to steal most were wanted posters right off the post office walls. They were always stapled to a bulletin board near the front door so I had to time the act of ripping one off just right so that I wouldn't be seen by anyone entering or leaving the building. Usually, the clerks were so busy weighing packages they didn't realize what was going on.

The strange thing about this ritual is that those old wanted posters somehow reminded me of movie stills, guys with guns in their hands, women whose long hair was a long dark slash across the eyes. Some of those wanted men might have been Humphrey Bogart or Jimmy Cagney or George Raft wannabes.

But, their eyes always seemed a little off center or cockeyed and the expressions on their faces were strangely frozen, maybe even a little grotesque, almost always fuck you. Maybe that's really why I liked them so much. These were the poses of bank robbers and murderers and they reminded me so much of men who lived from time to time at the Clifton Hotel.

I can no longer recall the names of the outlaws on those posters anymore. Maybe I was never so much interested in their names as I was in what they did, the mayhem they created. It's very possible that I stole a Willie Sutton handbill without realizing who he was. And, it seems as though I do recall seeing one of John Dillinger nailed on a wall somewhere.

Maybe, in the police station where my old man used to hang out when he wasn't on duty as a fireman. He more often than not had a bottle or a flask with him and he'd pass it around to the guys in the station and pretty soon everyone was feeling good. In those days, liquor was just part of a working cop or fireman's job.

I didn't know it then but I was going to meet the outlaw. And, the reason I didn't know it was I was also growing up around outlaws. They were everywhere, electric and anonymous. They were my old man's friends as well as his enemies. They were the drifters who slid off the freight cars down in the yards. They were the ex bootleggers who had become cops or low level gangsters who ran slots, back room poker games, or hookers in the neighborhood.

Yet, somehow stealing those wanted posters was my way of connecting gangster movies to the streets that I knew. The one thing I definitely figured out was the dark side even before George Lucas made it part of the lingo.

I met the outlaws long before I wrote my first story. And, many of my early stories were really about outlaws. They bled out in the movies that were always looping around just inside my shadow.

when my old

man was
sober we'd
walk down
town to
the illinois
sporting
goods him
w/his cig
arets me w/a
hershey bar
to stare at
the knives &
guns dis
played in
the window
my old man
wd push his
face very
close to the
glass where
the handguns
were then
he'd step
back & say
kid you
wanna know
america you
need a gun
in yr belt

Excerpt from the essay
All the dark histories and the memory of blood

Not long after my father died, I would have dreams of him coming back looking for his blood. He'd stand in the doorway and say *"Where's it at??"* And every time i would have to ask what he was looking for and he'd say *my* blood. I don't have it anymore and I want it back it felt good where it ran underneath my skin and I didn't realize it until it was all gone.

when my old

man cut him
self while
shaving w/ a
straight razor
i tried
catching
the blood
that was
dripping
to the sink
& down
on the floor
& the
second he
saw what
i was doing
he sd
what the
fuck are
you up to
& I sd
i'm just
trying to
save yr
blood he
was holding
a finger
over the
slit on his
cheek when
he laughed
& sd you
can't save
something
that's already
lost

Chapter 3

Lost at the Movies

"My Aunt Nancy told me that she and my dad did whatever they had to do to get money if they wanted things like candy or to go to the movies as the family never had enough spare change to give them. So, they did whatever they had to do to raise the cash – run scams, sell things, steal, etc.

Going to the movies was my dad's passion as a kid much as it would be later in life as well. He was big into art, all types, all forms, and really appreciated a good movie when he saw one. To him it was like reading a great poem, he got excited about it, it got his adrenaline going and most of all inspired him to write which he did quite a bit."
-- Theron Moore

"Usually they'd start out with cartoons which we liked and then when they were over you were supposed to leave but we just stayed there all day, it was great and it was a lot better than having to back to the apartment and life we had back at the Clifton. And during the summer theatres had air conditioning which our apartment didn't have, we just had a fan, so it was nice and cool there as well."
-- Nancy Weir

Neil Wilgus: Your work has been called noir poetry and you might even have invented the term. Can you talk about what noir poetry is, how it's done and who does it?

Todd Moore: Hitting the mother lode meant hitting my roots. And my roots had to do with that old falling down hotel, the drunks and outlaws who lived there, and the way I survived that whole life style for almost twelve years. That coupled with my love for the old black and white movies of the forties and fifties, pretty much defined the way I would write.

I used to live at the movies when I was a kid. Bogart, Cagney, Raft, were my heroes and movies like High Sierra, The Treasure of Sierra Madre, and White Heat became kind of like a way of looking at *things. So, when I finally fought my way back to writing, this was where I went, and this was the way I began to see things through the poems.*

And, I suppose that I was probably one of the first poets of my generation to come up with the phrase Noir Poetry. I was reading Dashiell Hammett, Raymond Chandler, and Jim Thompson. And, I had seen all of Sam Peckinpah's movies, my favorite was naturally "The Wild Bunch" so, Noir Poetry just seemed like a natural fit for me.

The Big Loco

I cut school to go see "*White Heat.*" I went with a kid called Stretch because he looked like somebody had tied ropes to his arms and legs and stretched him until they couldn't stretch him any farther. He was gaunt looking and appeared older than I was, but he actually was younger and that was okay because he claimed to be my big brother and that way nobody questioned us and we sat right down front with fat boxes of butter corn and tall cokes rich with ice and Stretch sat there going "*Fuck*" and rubbing his hands together every time Cagney shot a guy.

Little did I realize that by cutting school to see "*White Heat*" that I was actually going to school. But, it was a different kind of school. It was the school of the outlaw. It was the school of the desperado. Sitting there in that ripped up seat with the floor covered with decades of blackened candy, probably cum, and very likely a drop or two of blood.

It was the movies for chrissake. It was the place you went if you were fucked up or wanted to be fucked up or just wanted to escape from the ordinary and everlasting bullshit of trying to get from one day to the next.

If "*White heat*" gave me nothing else, it left me with a sense of what I'd like to call loco style and old Jimmy Cagney had it to the max. And, I've never seen anybody in the movies or even real life do loco the way Cagney did it. Somehow he raised the bar on the movie outlaw. There was only one Cody Jarrett. After Cagney did Cody, nobody else could. Though, I sometimes wonder if maybe Sean Penn could take a whirl at it. He might just be the one to pull it off.

But it has to be done from the inside out. You can't fake it. It has to come from the vein and the bone or it just doesn't mojo. The same thing goes for the outlaw poem. You're either an outlaw or you're a tourist and if the latter is the case, then amigo, go back to selling shoes, junk stock, or cemetery plots. It's just that simple.

After the movie was over, we'd go to Stretch's house where his old man would be slugging Jim Beam like it was water. I could either go there or end up at my house where my old man would be doing the same thing.

Besides, Stretch had an old man who liked to play with guns and it felt like a nice sequel to the movie. His old man had a little Colt 25 auto, a cheap 32, and a single action 45 that he claimed he got off a dead man in El Paso.

Each time he told the story it was good, but always different. He didn't look or sound anything like Cagney. Instead, he was more like a hill cracker out of Kentucky or Tennessee. But, that was okay, too, because sometime during my stay there he'd slam a pistol into my hand, smile so hard that one of his teeth would show at his upper lip, and say, this is all the truth there is, boy. Anything else is a goddam lie.

And, I'd look into the wreckage of his face and I'd see a little of Cody Jarrett's crazy. *"Go ahead"* he'd say. *"Run it around in your hand. That's it. Touching a gun is like copping a feel. It stays with you, gets down inside you, makes you a little edgy."*

Then Stretch would crowd in and the old man would shove a gun into his hand, too, and he'd give me the look like see i got one too which means i am somebody and the two of us would walk around the room like we were getting ready to go down to the OK Corral or someplace.

Outlaw poetry comes out of Cagney's loco, Stretch and his old man, their guns, the crazy dreams you get at the movies, the crazy dreams you get just thinking about certain kinds of movies, the sense of being marginalized and not being able to do anything about it, the desperado ache to somehow through a violent ritual of absolution become someone or something better.

Or, if not that, then maybe just maybe it might just be possible to write the last best and greatest outlaw poem of all. A murder ballad dedicated to a darkly murderous republic.

Excerpt from the essay
The Images of Lethal Desire

Going to the movies, especially the gangster and cowboy movies where guys got killed but not for real, it felt like the stories I had going in my head. With some of the lines repeated or if they weren't, I repeated them and that made them feel better. And, then going to that gun store put all those feelings of death back into my eyes like a fresh shot of something I had to have there.

The big death lived there as well. It was bigger than anything in the movies. In those days, when a guy got shot at the movies there was never any blood. And I was always looking for wounds on the dead guys but I never saw any. Friends I was with would say *"It's a movie for chrissake,"* but if it was death it should show some blood. I was certain of that.

I was also certain that all those guns in the gun store were secretly inscribed with all the names that death ever had. Sure, it was a dream, but it also was real, as real as the silent poems I used to make up with the repeated lines going.

This was really the poem I put everything into. I had all my friends in there and all the movies that I went to and the names of all the rivers I knew and my father was there with his beaten up typewriter and his bottle of whiskey and all the street names were there and my father's alkie friends and the hookers.

All the forms of death that I've ever known or imagined were there in the little pieces of broken beer bottle glass in the gutter, and they were there in the discarded hubcaps, and they were there in the flat tires in the vacant lots, and they were there in empty cigarette packs thrown into the gravel, and they were there in the bent nails tossed into the weeds.

But, those guns in that gun store., they formed a special cluster of images I could never get rid of. They still swim around in all of my dreams, and, I always go back there when I need a gun for one of my poems. I guess you could call them my little images of lethal desire.

Excerpt from the essay
The Dark Side of America

I used to get the old movie stills mixed up with the photographs of real outlaws. The lobbies of the movie theaters in town were loaded with movie stills from the thirties and forties and it was a little ritual of mine to stop before each one like I was pausing before the stations of the cross.

The kid I was going to the movies with would yell *"Come on for chrissake we'll miss the previews."*

I'd yell back, *"We'll see them after the movie because I'm gonna have to sit through this one twice."*

I did that with *"White Heat," "The Treasure of the Sierra Madre," "The Asphalt Jungle" "Kiss of Death," "The Maltese Falcon," "The Big Sleep,"* and I don't know how many others.

Once, some kid said to me, *"Why would you ever wanna see any movie twice?"* and my reply was, *"Why wouldn't I?"* It just seemed natural like learning to dream or stealing something and crime was like breathing, maybe the most natural thing of all.

We always had guns. Toy ones at first. BB guns next, and then the real ones. My old man would never let me have one but I had friends who found ways. The best place to go to shoot anything was down to the river or across that black water to the city dump where the rats were almost as big as small dogs and the shooting was easy and Lucky had a 22 revolver I forget the make I think it was one of those midnight specials and we would shoot at anything that moved in the garbage.

I remember once watching a guy shoot the back legs off a feral dog with a 12 gauge shotgun. Somehow the dog got away in the underbrush and the guy kept saying, could you believe all that blood. I never told him but I always believed blood. Blood never lies.

Even in those old black and white movies where they didn't show much blood, I believed in blood because in those days blood was all we had. A wino is sitting on the pavement behind the hotel. I walk outside and he looks up and smiles and says, *"This is good shit would you like to try a little?"* My father had a battle with the bottle and I hated it, so I tell the wino no.

Just twenty feet away the fire barrel is going and the flames are flying up several feet above the rim of the barrel and the wino says, *"My soul is in there. But you know what, I can't feel it burning. "*Then he adds, *"See all that green in the black smoke, that's the color of a soul when it's on fire."*

When I was twelve I'd see a movie still of Bogart and think it was Dillinger, and, in a book, I'd see a photograph of Dillinger and think it was Bogart. It was easy to do they could have been brothers.

Even when I finally realized that Dillinger never made any movies and Bogart never robbed any banks, I thought to myself that they should have, that maybe in some alternate universe each man had lived the other man's life and that thought somehow made me feel good.

I always liked watching *"Shane"* but I never really liked Alan Ladd for the part. He didn't fit my idea of a gunfighter I don't know why. The role had a dark side that doesn't show up that much in the movie. And, yeah, I know Shane is really the ideal gunfighter, but I wanted him to be the un-ideal. I wanted him to be darker than that.

I used to think that Jack Palance should have played Shane. Palance was total dark side, the way he looked with that gaunt almost skeleton like skull face. To me, that was Shane.

You couldn't really like a man like that for a hero but you could somehow be drawn to him as a gunfighter.

And, for Wilson I would have picked either Richard Widmark or Dan Duryea. They both were always bad to the bone, perfect for the bad guy and can you imagine that last shootout in Ryker's Saloon with Palance mowing them all down.

No, you couldn't love Palance or even like him. He was too dark for that but he was just dark enough to be a stone cold killer who happened to want to help out some farmers on a whim, shoot down all the villains who needed shooting down and then ride out into the night as though he was really part of the night. Because America's killers are really part of the night, they belong to the night. They belong to the moon.

I remember some nights going to a gangster movie or maybe it was a double bill, Bogart and Cagney, or maybe it was George Raft and Dane Clark and there was always a shootout.

A lot of times they were using machine guns and the sounds of those guns going off always got to me, got me so nervous I couldn't get to sleep, and then the lights were off and my old man was snoring and I could hear the rat in the hole in the wall above my old rickety fold up bed.

I could hear the way his little claws were going over rotten wood and I would lie perfectly still and think he's staring at me, I can feel his eyes going all over me. I never got him but I wanted to, I wanted to kill that rat more than anything else but when that hole got plugged up I know he went somewhere else in the hotel's walls.

I just know that he escaped and was in there waiting and you wouldn't be able to see him even if you could somehow crawl into the space of that wall, maybe all you would be able to see were his eyes. The thought of his eyes went straight through me. I wanted to get him in the eyes because I knew that his soul wasn't too far away…

Chapter 4

Killin' Time with the Angel of Death

& death

had a way
of speaking
in tongues
down by the
river where the
black horse
drowned &
jerry sd one
minute his
old man was
talking abt
hank aaron
& the next he
was blowing
his brains
all over
the wall w/
his lucky 32
jerry never
blinked
when he sd
it looked like
white boogers
pimpling the
blood & we
laughed when
the hooker
kept hanging
her head out
of the 2nd
floor window

of the clifton
hotel yelling
2 bucks to
see the wood
chuck boys &
the horse doc
tor who used
to sit on a
wooden chair
outside his
office next
to raineys
café liked to
scare us by
saying he'd
seen death
ride in on a
big palomino
& kenny who
never showed
any fear sd
well wd you
& death like
to suck my
dick & when
i traded the
railroad badge
my old man
kept in his
brown suit
coat pocket
for a big
switchblade
he went crazy
cuz he cdn't
find it &
sailed an
ashtray in the
shape of wyo
ming off

the beaten
up dresser
sd it was
the only
thing he had
that belonged
to his father
that his
history was
gone in the
railroad soot
of the lost july
wind which
brought the
rotting smell
of shit meat
& rags on
fire & my
old man wd
sit in the
dark drinking
calvert out
of a cracked
water glass
& say i'm not
afraid to die
but i've seen
death taking a
piss in the
toilet & he's
in there now
all bone white
just waiting
for me &
when i went
to shoot ray's
22 down by
the stockpens
i saw a guy
trying to stick

a gray pony
w/a long ice
pick & he
& the nag
went down
in a tangle
& he ended up
w/the pick in
his leg & the
old railroad
cop called
jake brushed
a fleck of dirt
off the pistol
butt stuck his
belt & sd boys
you know it's
bad luck to
mess around w/
this river it's
the drowning
water &
death speaks
in tongues

Excerpt from the essay
Betting with Blood

When I was a kid I used to watch men in the alley throw dice off a wall and rake in the money. Some of them held twenty dollar bills folded lengthwise between their fingers. I loved the style of that and I loved the way they'd yell when they won and swore when they lost. I loved the way they bet hard, won big, and lost everything when they finally lost.

And, the reason why I loved watching these guys play was because it was visceral, immediate, and often violent. It almost felt like I was being slammed against bricks. The action was straight from the gut with lots of gravel kicking, fists going, and whiskey chugged. The whole thing was as good as a movie. Maybe better.

Cobb used to walk straight toward the local gangster. Everyone knew the man was connected but he was old and looked more like a priest than a killer. Cobb would take advantage of that and make it look like he was going to walk right into the gangster, except that the gangster had an ex-wrestler body guard called Pinball who would run interference for when he had to.

The body guard would give Cobb a shove and the gangster would say out of the side of his mouth, "*You like walking on those legs?*" Cobb always laughed while he picked himself up off the sidewalk.

Then I'd say, "Come *on Cobb, you trying to get yourself killed?*" Cobb would get a loony grin on his face and say, "*You gotta walk the man down to know you're alive.*"

Once I watched my old man deal himself and an empty chair a poker hand. When he'd dealt himself five cards, I said *"Pop, there's no one sitting in that chair."*

My old man poured himself a tall shot, drank it, and said, "*Wrong. Death is sitting in that chair. I'm playing a game of five card stud with Death.*"

I looked at my old man's hand. Then I looked at Death's hand. My old man had three aces. Death was holding three sevens.

I said, "*You win.*"

My old man turned Death's hand face up and said, "*Wrong again. Death wins.*"

I said, "*You're holding three aces to Death's three sevens.* "

"Yeah," my old man replied. *"But the thing you have to realize is that even though you may be holding the good cards, Death will always beat you, always and forever."*

Then he poured himself another shot, laughed, and gave the empty chair the finger.

"I thought I was a goner for sure that time those hit men held me in that hotel room over night," my old man said.

"How come they grabbed you?" I asked.

"Skimming the bag money only it wasn't me but the guy I worked for."

It didn't take long for them to break him.

"The one killer wanted to cut my fingers off. The other said, too fucken messy. Lets break one. The bone crack made the tears come to my eyes. The one who wanted to cut my fingers off said, I'm gonna deal you a card. If it's even you live, odd you die.

I always used to draw to a lucky number seven. It was my juice card, magic to my eyes. I watched this guy toss one across the table. It seemed like it took forever to land. Pick it up, the guy said, cocking and uncocking his revolver.

I waited a few seconds, then dragged it across, still not looking at it. You gonna turn it over or not. I decided to turn it up quick, sudden death style. It was an eight. Goddam lucky for you motherfucker. He gave me a bitch slap across the face, laughed, and then they left."

Excerpt from the essay
The Dangerous Business

How many murders have I actually seen? The truth is, I heard one once, and, never wanted to hear that shit again. I heard a woman being strangled with a toaster cord and I thought this guy was just beating his wife up like a lot of guys did then. Later, I found out the truth and it has haunted me the way that the dark waters of war, murder, and executions haunted Goya.

And, how much violence have I seen? I nearly killed a kid with a brick once. I've been in two knife fights with only minor scratches from each one. Stupid, very stupid, but part of the way I was living fifty years ago. I also saw the corpse of one man after he hanged himself. Didn't get a good look at his face, but his hands were blue, and those blue hands have been with me a very long time.

the dutchman

lived in room
303 he re
quested it
because of
the two 3's
w/a void
in between
he wore
a pork pie
hat chewed
juicy fruit
gum & paid
me a buck
to go out
for his
coffee which
had to have
3 tea spoons
of sugar
he smelled
of sweet
aftershave
& flesh
that was
rotting
one night
he told me
he was
death's ven
triloquist
then pulled
out his 45
auto to ask
abt the rain
the wind
& the wea
ther in hell

Excerpt from the essay
All the Dark Talking to the Angel of Death

When I was a kid I remember watching an old alkie dancing with himself and humming strangely out by the fire barrel behind the Clifton Hotel. It was like he was saying words but I couldn't make them out. It was like he was using dark words overlaid with more dark words. I'd only been watching him for just a few minutes when he stopped, staggered a few steps toward me and said, *"What are you staring at?"* He looked as though he had just risen from the dead.

When I didn't reply, he pulled a bottle of vodka out of his back pocket and took a swallow. *"I don't like people watching while I do my little dance with the angel of death."*

"I don't see any angel of death," I said. He smiled and it almost looked like a dark moth flew out of his mouth.

He said, *"You never see the angel of death, but it sees you. It sees you all over in the night of your being."*

Three days later my old man found the alkie dead in his room. His mouth was wide open as though surprised by some kind of phantom talking.

Sleeping with the Angel of Death

I'll never forget the day I went to see an old bootlegger die. He went by the name of Whitey Fallon but my old man said it was only an alias. That this guy lived by many names, that nobody really knew who the hell he was.

I stood in the doorway watching a black widow spider crawl toward the ceiling while my old man sat on the edge of Fallon's bed talking low.

Finally, Fallon said, *"Promise?"* and my old man said, *"Promise"* and that was that.

Fallon sat up and spit a mouthful of phlegm and blood into dark coffee can placed next to the bed.

"You belong in a hospital," my old man said, moving toward the door. *"Fuck'em,"* Fallon replied, getting the sound of everything boiling way down in his lungs.

Just before my old man reached the door, Fallon said, *"You ever sleep with the angel of death?"*

"The what?" my old man asked.

"The angel of death" Fallon replied, spitting again.

"Not that I recall" my old man replied.

"Everybody gets a turn" Fallon said. *"She's smooth as silk and one helluva lay."*

Those times Shorty and I went down to the river to shoot birds and snakes we'd see an old woman come out of the high grass and trees across the river and wave. She'd just stand there and wave and wave for the longest time.

"Who the hell is she?" Shorty asked once.

"You don't know?" I said. *"They call her Night Water Mary. Her son drowned somewhere around here fifty years ago and she's been searching for him ever since."*

Shorty said," *Should I put a slug past her ear?"*

"Fuck no," I replied. *"She might be crazy but I don't wanna kill her."*

Shorty stuck his gun hand out and I grabbed it, jamming the pistol barrel skyward toward the prodigal outlaw moon.

"Goddamit, no!" I yelled.

Shorty gave me one of his skin and bone smiles and whispered, *"Motherfucker."* He said it with a whole lot of spin in his breath. When we left, Night Water Mary was still waving across the black river.

Some years before he died, Bill Gersh did a whole series of prints featuring a dark woman. They were collages of mostly broken images. Old adobe houses, Tony Moffeit playing a drum, fragments of a woman's hand, the fingers, and the lure of those finger parts.

But, it was the woman's face or the broken parts of it, which fascinated and obsessed me. In the framed print I own, the dark woman's lips are visible. But a black Rothko like cloud obscures her eyes.

Every time I stare at this print I think of Whitey Fallon and his angel of death. And, I stare at it every day before writing a poem. Call it a ritual for good luck, call it dreaming the skin dream that lives at the center of every duende, call it the french kiss energy that conjures every good poem.

And, I am also reminded of the way that Anna Sage must have looked to Dillinger the last night of his life. There she was, standing beneath the marquee of the Biograph Theater in that bright orange dress that turned blood red in the glare of those movie theater lights.

The way the dress bled out into the ninety degree night, the way that Dillinger must have felt her hot moist body move under those sizzling kliegs, the way she had to have smiled at him with all of her heavy cunt sweat and his massive desire.

Dickie Boy's mother was one of the biggest women I have ever known. She never washed and when the wind would bring her odor toward me, it was unbearable even though I made it a habit of not standing too close.

And, it wasn't just the smell that got me. She liked to walk around with a butcher knife in her hand. Whenever Dickie Boy did something she didn't like, she'd aim the blade at him and smile. That was all it took to back Dickie Boy off.

Every once in awhile she'd get mad at Dickie Boy's old man and would chase him around the house with the butcher knife. She never caught him but it was a show.

Her large breasts would come boiling out of her dress which was unbuttoned at the top and they would flail the wind while she pounded through the yard, her knife slicing the air all around her.

Sometimes she would look over in my direction and yell some fierce half swallowed word. Her face was a map of embattled fat.

But those death angels aren't all fat. How about the platinum and steel hard image of Barbara Stanwyk in "*Double Indemnity*," or Mercedes McCambridge in "*Johnny Guitar*" or Sharon Stone in "*Basic*

Instinct?" How about Glenn Close in "Fatal *Attraction?*" How about Bette Davis in almost anything?

The duende can't exist without the presence of the angel of death. She is always on stage during a reading and she is always at your shoulder when the black wind of the duende parts the curtains and the poem appears. She is always there with her butcher knife and her chrome plated automatic. She wants nothing less than your words, your breath, your blood and your love. No great poetry exists without her.

The spirit of the angel of death informs almost anything written, sculpted, painted, danced, or sung. Where there are words, there is also silence. Where there is a block of stone to be shaped, there is also emptiness, the abyss. Where there is a canvas waiting for the paint, there is also a gray door opening into the void. Where there is a space aching to be danced in, there is also oblivion, longing only for other forms of oblivion. And, where there is singing, there are also the sounds of wreckage and nothing.

The only true enemy of the angel of death is the outlaw poet. And, he is the enemy because he knows that the wages for writing poetry are sleeping with her. It is an existential decision he must make if he wants to be an outlaw and a poet. There is no other way. The wages of fear means you have declined the offer. You sleep only with nightmares, disease, demons, and regret. The wages of poetry lie in the burnt meat of the void and the transcendent spark of the word. The angel of death is waiting.

Chapter 5

Blood on the Streets

Excerpt from the essay
Nightmare Frenzy

Kenny G. wasn't looking for a blackjack in the face. He was the kind of guy who wanted to talk shit to you before he kicked your ass. He wanted to scare you by telling you what he was going to do to you, high and low.

Maybe if you just took it, he'd give you a fat lip and let you go with a warning. Or, maybe he'd just beat the living hell out of you for the fun of it just to watch you yell. Then he'd go from there to giving you a shove or punching you hard in the chest or guts. It was his idea of fight foreplay.

So, the blackjack surprised him. Surprised and hurt him both at the same time. I'd found it down in the Illinois Central rail yards between two freight cars. It was stamped Illinois Central Railroad on one side and had some initials on the other. I figure some railroad cop had accidentally dropped it and suddenly it was my lucky day if you can call a tool made specifically for crunching bones luck.

The best advice I ever got from my old man was when you hit a guy, give it to him straight in the face and make it hard. As hard as you ever hit anything because when you land a punch in the face just right the pain radiates everywhere. And, it really fucks up the eyes. So, that's where I hit Kenny G. with that jack.

He was still talking when I swung and the sound it made was like a hammer sinking into meat. Kenny G. finished his sentence spitting by out a tooth and a whole lot of blood. And, while he was bent in half, I hit him again. A drunk coming out of The Rainbow Tap I was standing in front of said, you didn't give him a chance. And, I said, he didn't deserve one. I had let him become one of my demons until I caught his blood in my hands.

sitting over

coffee in the
clifton café
when waco
shoved the
oblong pack
age across
the table he
grinned &
sd open it
when i
ripped
the butcher
paper
the first
thing i saw
was the
brown lea
ther grip
of a black
jack merry
xmas he sd
rubbing the
scar on his
cheek i used
it on milo
the bones in
his nose
snapped like
sticks in a
sack

you look like

a man who's
afraid to
die graham
sd sitting
down at the
table in the
clifton café
my old man
spit some
thing green
in his cof
fee then
looked at
graham
who sd
you'll be
spitting
more than
phlegm if
you fuck
w/the deal
what deal
my old
man asked
taking the
fifty graham
put on the
table a 45
auto showed
under his
coat

Excerpt from the essay
Poetry, Guns and the Outlaw Self

The night Jerry G. caught me with a hard left hook I was acting cocky like I owned the street and everything that walked there. Jerry was a squirt, a little guy I thought I had the edge on. I had no idea a little guy could pack such a punch, and,I even saw it coming. It was almost perfect the way his arm and fist shot away from his body and I was both hypnotized and scared shitless of the speed.

I knew this kid who had the Tommy Udo laugh down. I didn't even have to see him. All I had to do was hear that laugh. For years, I tried to get that laugh into a poem. I could even see this kid's face and then Richard Widmark's face and after awhile it was like their faces had grown into each other because of the laugh.

It was almost like that laugh permanently part of them both and I couldn't think of one without the other and the laugh was kind of like a sound scar that got into both of them. It was like a wound that they both reenacted.

Lee Shanley used to hang around the Illinois Central yards. He was a couple years ahead of me in school when he dropped out to work construction. After awhile he got tired of that and just did odd jobs for guys he knew in town.

Once, when I saw the blackjack in his back pocket I said, "*Is that part of your work?*"

He smiled and replied "*I like the way it feels there.*" Once when I caught him reading a copy of <u>The Big Sleep</u>, I said, "*So what does the title mean?*"

And, he said, "*Death kid and death don't mean a thing.*"

Excerpt from the essay
Taking on Bukowski

When I was a kid I used to know a guy who was good with his fists. In fact, I never saw anyone up close as good as he was. He had the footwork, a regular Gene Kelly, he could dance just beyond anyone's right cross, he never got caught in an upper cut trap. He could see a left coming from a block away. But the real magic was in his fists.

He worked them the way Picasso worked the paint brushes, he worked them the way Houdini did padlocks, he worked them the way Hemingway worked the shotguns. And, this guy took on the neighborhood and the best part of it was there was no one who could take him.

The only problem was he was a sucker for the easy score. He got caught up in some kind of stick up and got sent to the pen. After that I lost track of him. But while he lasted he was good, he was the best I'd ever seen.

Excerpt from the essay
Sign of the Outlaw

When I was a kid I remember my old man standing in the doorway of one of his favorite watering holes, a dive called Jerry's. He was telling Jerry who was tending bar one of his outrageous stories. I think it was the one where he and some other guy went hunting for The Lost Dutchman Mine in Arizona back in the Twenties.

When he got done Jerry looked up from the draft he was pouring and gave my old man the finger. He did it with a smile and to complete the ritual, my old man returned the favor. Then the whole joint went up in laughter and Jerry bought the next round for the house.

I was fighting a kid down by the railroad tracks. He was trying to get me with a railroad spike and I had a cut down lead pipe and he grazed me once in the side scraping my ribcage and I got him a good one just above the left ear and he dropped the spike and took off across the tracks. When he got to the other side, he stopped next to a Southern Pacific boxcar and flipped me off before taking off for the hobo jungle down by the river.

My old man used to tell me to be careful about who I was giving the finger to. He said he used to know a gambler back in the Twenties who would cut the middle fingers off guys who had flipped him off. My old man grinned when he told me the story because once when this gambler's house caught fire, my old man helped carry some of this guy's suitcases out of the house.

Later, the gambler took my old man aside and said, *"Don't ever tell anyone I showed you this shit."*

He opened one of the suitcases and ran his hand over bundles of tens and twenty dollar bills. Then he peeled a couple off a stack and gave them to my old man who said, *"I'm a fireman, it's my job."*

"Go on and take it" the gambler said. *"And, you can have this, too."*

He dropped a couple of finger bones into my old man's hand, then smiled and said, *"Don't ask."*

Excerpt from the essay
I write in the blood

Maybe the best fistfight I ever saw happened in front of the Clifton Hotel. Two drunken section hands got into it in the grass strip out in front of the hotel and each time one of them connected with a hard right or a quick left I could hear the sound of knuckles on meat and pretty soon both of them were starting to bleed and when they got out on the sidewalk and were stagger dancing around each other some of their blood went down on the sidewalk.

I don't remember who won. Maybe they both stopped out of sheer pain and exhaustion. I know they both headed for the bar just a block away. I also know that my old man walked over and put his shoe in the blood.

I said, *"What did you do that for?"*

He replied, "*I want to wear their blood because it's good for the dreams."*

Excerpt from essay
Machine Guns, Movies, Culture and Dreams

"While I was on the fire department it was the bloodiest thing I ever saw", my old man said, studying a shot glass filled almost to the rim with whiskey.

Someone had killed this guy down by the old vinegar works and dumped him out in the middle of the street. He must've had half a dozen slugs in his chest. His neck tie was nearly cut in half.

The cop in charge told the newspaper reporter, *"We're gonna call this one a suicide."*

The reporter stepped back, said, *"Somebody mowed this man down with a machine gun."*

The cop smiled, hawked up a big gob of yellow spit and sent it next to the dead man's face. He said it again. *"Suicide."*

The news photographer motioned the reporter off to the side and said, *"Let's don't get in the middle of this."*

"How come?" the reporter asked?

The photographer leaned in and said, *"Where machine guns are involved its mob shit. You start asking around, we'll both have blood out the ass. Like this poor bastard."*

I'm twelve years old, standing at the main desk in the Clifton Hotel where my old man is the night clerk and he's talking to a man who calls himself the freelancer.

"I Remember from back in the old days when I used to ride the suicide seat in a scout car for Keeler," the guy says.

My old man grins and says, *"He was the only legger who tried to compete   with   Capone."*

The freelancer laughs, says, *"Nobody ever found his body."*

"You still have that Thompson you carried back then?" my old man asks.

"It's *in a canvas bag, the trunk of my car. These days you never know."*

My old man tapped some Bull Durham into a cigarette paper, sealed it shut with his tongue and said, "Would *it be bad form to ask if you ever used it?"*

The freelancer paused and then cracked a smile. *"Yeah, bad form."*

The smile partly went away when he said, *"It's the gun that America is all about."*

My old man nodded and said, *"The American Dream."*

Excerpt from the essay
Walking Around in the Blood

Kenny showed me the rock he'd hit his old man in the head with. He said the old man was still breathing when he left. We were standing on the banks of the Kish when he looked at me and said, *"Think I should I throw it in?"*

I said, *"His blood is still on it."*

He wiped the blood off on his shirt. *"Now do you think it's alright to throw it in?"*

I looked over at him. *"It doesn't matter if you throw it in or not. You will always have it. It's part of you now."*

He sat down in the weeds on the riverbank and started pounding the ground with the rock. But the blood was still there. It stains you, imprints you, tattoos you.

Once at the Clifton Hotel I remember my old man pointing to a patch of grass under the big cottonwood tree at the front of the hotel and saying, *"For god's sake don't ever walk there. That's where Texas Jack*

Paterson blew his brains out back in the late thirties. I should know, I was on the fire department then and had to help clean up the mess. Some of his brains went out into the street and got black from the car tires."

When he finished telling the story I walked through that patch of grass just to see how it would feel and my old man said, *"Now, you've got his blood on you and it will never come off. "*

I checked my shoes just to be sure there was no blood on them. The funny thing, though, every time I walked by that patch of grass I would always check my shoes. Even now, in some of my dreams I catch myself wearing some of Texas Jack's blood.

You can't be an Outlaw without wearing the blood. Or tasting it for that matter....

Tasting the Blood

I found the blackjack just a few yards away from a railroad switch. It was lying right out in the cinders like it had just been dropped. I picked it up and slapped the jack head into the palm of my hand. The impact stung my skin and made the bones in the palm of my hand ache. I looked up and down the tracks to make sure nobody saw me pick it up. Then I walked down through the weeds and then through a hobo jungle before ducking underneath the old railroad bridge where I could get a better look at the jack.

It was all black, had some wear on the grip and some nicks and dings in the slick hard leather on both sides of the head. Also, on one side scratched in the leather was the word Whiskey and the words I think I killed. The rest of the sentence was either worn out or simply left incomplete. I slipped my hand into the knuckle band and let the leaded weight of the jack drag my hand down a little.

When I showed the jack to Jerry he said, *"How much do you want for it?"*

At first, I didn't want to sell it. I liked the way it felt when I swung it around and I liked the way it bumped against my leg when I slid it into my right front pocket. But Jerry kept saying, *"I gotta have it, I gotta have it."*

His old man was in the next room sleeping off an all night drunk and I was afraid Jerry would wake him up. He was a dangerous man, sober or drunk.

Finally, Jerry threw a switchblade and a five dollar bill on the table and said, *"With that I can kick the shit out of the old man any day of the week. Come on, let's trade."*

"I'll think about it," I said. I watched Jerry's face fold up somewhere between a frown and sheer rage.

"Okay" he said. *"But I wanna do something."*

"Like what?" I asked.

"Let's go down and see Frankie."

"Frankie will kick the living shit out of you and then he'll start in on me" I replied. hefting the jack.

"Not with that he won't. Why don't we break it in on Frankie" Jerry said. He smiled and the white scar on the right side of his face smiled, too.

We found Frankie sitting on a bench outside Reno's Billiards. He was reading a Batman comic book and only looked up when he heard the steel clips on the bottoms of Jerry's shoes clicking on the pavement.

Frankie put the comic book down and said, *"You coming back for more of the same?"*

Frankie had one eye. He'd lost the right when somebody had smashed a long neck beer bottle across his face and a sliver had stuck in his eye.

Jerry waited for Frankie to come in close. Frankie's main thing was to get you around the neck with his left arm and then deliver half a dozen cheek breaking blows with his right. I'd seen him fight before and he always operated the same way. He was big enough and strong enough and never had to change his tactics.

As soon as Frankie hooked that arm out to make a grab, Jerry ducked in and slammed Frankie hard in the face with the jack. I heard it connect. It sounded like something crunching underfoot. Frankie stepped back, almost stumbling. He had his right hand up to his face and there was blood at the corner of his mouth.

"You motherfucker" Frankie said. The words came out of him like a low growl.

When Frankie rushed in, Jerry was ready. He meant to hit Frankie in the nose. I remember once when his old man was trying to tell us how to fight:

"Go for the nose" he said, lunging around the room drunkenly with his fists held out against the black air. *"The nose is what you wanna break. Shatter the nose."*

Jerry's blow caught Frankie just above the right ear and mussed up his ducktail and he almost went down but caught himself on the sidewalk. When he stood up he had a thin streak of blood starting to come out of his hair. Jerry was laughing and that really got Frankie. The laughter that came out of Jerry was thin and high pitched, just this side of a howl.

Frankie said, "*Now, I'm gonna kill you real good.*"

He walked toward Jerry with both hands out. He was big and his hands were big and the blood on his face gave him a spooky, desperate, broken look. Jerry stepped back from the first roundhouse and then walked in swinging the jack from high up, bringing it down hard across the middle of Frankie's face.

I'd heard that sound before. It sounded like my old man's razor strop when it landed. Frankie was just starting to fall sideways and Jerry was right there hitting him again and again. He gave him one in the jaw, one across the eyes and one in the ear.

Frankie was still in midair when a guy called Crackers ran out of the pool hall and grabbed Jerry from behind. By this time Frankie was sitting on the sidewalk with the blood coming down his face in three streams. He was trying to get up but his legs wouldn't work and after a couple of tries he just stayed there, shaking his head, with the blood going in all directions.

When Jerry broke free of Crackers the blackjack came out of his hand and bounced once on the sewer drain before it rolled through the opening in the iron grate and splashed in the gutter water below.

Crackers looked over at Frankie who was still shaking the blood off his face and said, "*You want me to call the cops?*"

"*What??*" Frankie said, trying to get hold of a parking meter so he could stand up.

"I said do you want me to call the cops?"

"*Fuck the cops*" Frankie said. "*No cops*"

"*Okay*" Crackers replied. "*But you little fuckers better take this shit down the street before I change my mind*"

Jerry winked at me and we walked a block to the movies. An old double bill of George Raft gangster films were playing and the usher knew us and let us slip in for free.

I bought a large coke and popcorn. Jerry said he wasn't hungry and then ate half of my popcorn anyway.

There was a scene where Raft uses a 45 auto to pistol whip a guy and Jerry said, "*See that?*" He was shaking all over. Then Jerry leaned close and said, "*I tasted his blood.*"

I leaned over and said, *"You know what? I did the same thing. It was good."*

Blood in, Blood out

When i was a kid, I remember my grandmother telling me a story that had a cowboy riding out of town with blood on his arm. She never exactly said how he got it, maybe from being shot or stabbed or maybe he'd been hurt in an accident and was riding back to camp to get it bandaged up.

She did distinctly remember a cowboy riding out of town with blood on his arm and I remember the way that she told it. That wavering, partly squeaky, halting voice of hers and the picture i got from it of the way that cowboy looked, certainly desolate and definitely broken as he rode from town.

Then I recall watching a fistfight that involved a friend of mine called Shorty and another kid called Peewee and Peewee was an artist when it came to using his fists. Left right left and Shorty went down. That happened half a dozen times till his old man came over and said you got any blood on you. Shorty said no so his old man said you can't quite till you get some blood on you.

After the railroad cop shot the stray dog, he went over like he was going to stroke its fur but instead he stuck his finger in the bullet wound and pulled it out. Then he glanced over at me and said candy for the baby.

Blood in, blood out

Dead Stupid, Wise Blood

Lonnie's old man was beating the shit out of him and I just stood over on the railroad tracks and watched. When I saw how bloody Lonnie's mouth was getting I picked a big stone out of the cinders and passed it back and forth from hand to hand.

Lonnie's old man glanced over at me, laughed, and said, *"When I get done with this sack of shit I'll start on you."*

"Run" Lonnie yelled. *"You gotta run."*

I liked to sleep with a blackjack. I knocked it out of a kid's hand with a two by four and then it was mine. My old man didn't know about it or he would have traded it in at one of the local bars for a bottle of whiskey.

It felt good to sleep with it because I could always reach for it in the dark and I knew that if the rat in the hole above my bed ever came out I could kill it. Just touching it under my pillow was enough to make me feel good.

Shorty pulled a 22 revolver out of his pocket. I thought he was bullshitting me since it looked like a cap pistol. He looked over at me and said, *"Christ no, it's the real thing."*

"Prove it."

We went down to the railroad tracks where he shot a crow sitting on a tree limb and when the blood came out of the crow's darkness Shorty let me hold revolver and I said *"Where did you get it?"*

Shorty just smiled and then he took the gun back and dipped the barrel into the crow's blood. He said he'd seen that done in a movie that you had to do that to make it all good.

We were all outlaws then and i think we were poets too. We would have admitted to being outlaws. After all, Bogart was an outlaw. Everyone knew he was a movie star, but he was an outlaw underneath it all. Kirk Douglas was an outlaw. Everyone knew he was a movie star too, but you didn't dress like that and you didn't talk like that and you didn't look like that unless you were an outlaw.

We were all outlaws pretending to be Humphrey Bogart and Kirk Douglas and Jimmy Cagney but we were just street thieves walking around with maybe a pack of cigarettes, a dollar in change if we were lucky, and a switchblade knife to make it all good.

You had to have a switchblade knife. And, you had to walk around like you were somebody even though you were probably nobody and headed to prison in the future for a gas station stick up or an offhand murder. The river knew that, the railroad tracks knew that, the hobo woods knew that.

You were on a fast track to alcoholism, prison, or a violent death. But, somehow those noir movies and those outlaw actors made it all better.

In those days, when you knew something you knew it in the blood. You had to. You either were dead stupid and were forever a mark on the street or you were wise, wise in the blood.

frankie put

the cigaret
out in
his hand
sd i
think yr
fucken w/
me nick
sd i'd
never do
that he
was
smiling
all around
his cigaret
when he
put the
25 auto
out on
the table
frankie sd
got any
plans on
how yr
gonna
take a
shit when
i stick
that pea
shooter up
yr ass

Chapter 6

Tommy Gun Blues

guns

reno sd
handing his
38 butt
first to my
old man
who stuck
it in his
belt &
walked
around the
room like
he was one
of the
gunfighters
from his
failed
western it
ain't like
that reno
sd snapping
his fingers
to get the
gun back
it's like this
he walked
over to me
stuck the
gun in my
ribs & went
bang it's
like that

& it's any
thing but
clean

we cut

thru the
railyard
& headed
straight
for the
river bridge
where we
stopped
in the
middle
my old
man sd
you gotta
be my
eyes &
took the
.38 out
of his
pocket
how much
you getting
paid to
dump it
I sd 50
he replied
look at it
he sd his
spider
hands
crawling
all over it
a real 38
smith &

wesson
murder &
class he
sd murder
& class
then let
it go into
the river

when my old

man was
sober we'd
walk down
town to
the Illinois
sporting
goods him
w/ his cig
arets me w/ a
hershey bar
to stare at
the knives &
guns dis
played in
the window
my old man
wd push his
face very
close to the
glass where
the handguns
were then
he'd step
back & say
kid you
wanna know
america you
need a gun
in yr belt

playing guns

behind the
clifton hotel
frankie has
the roy rogers
w/the crack
in the plastic
long horn
grip i have
the gene autry
& we're just
getting ready
to step out
in the alley
for a classic
showdown
when this
guy gets out
of a black
ford & walks
over sez you
boys ever
see a real
gun he's
chewing
bubble gum
& every once
in awhile
blows a big
one that gets
stuck to his
face then a
voice in the
car yells hey
shithead
bubble gum
sez i was just
gonna & the
voice in the

car sez don't
before he turns
to go bubble
gum flashes a
pistol butt
inside his coat
sez bang
yr dead

The Spirit Gun and the Dream of America

Some nights when the mountain lightning is throwing flashes all over my bedroom I can almost hear someone breathing in the next room. The traffic outside interrupts the spaced breaths. Then after awhile it starts in again, so I reach underneath my bed for the smooth grip on the 22 mag, haul it out, thumb the safety off, walk to the next room, and switch on the light, but nobody's there.

Somebody's there alright but nobody's there. I'd like to think the nobody who is there is John Dillinger. I'd like to think that Dillinger is secretly living in my house and this makes it easier for me to conjure him into a poem.

I'd like to think Dillinger is sitting on the edge of the bed with the machine gun straddled across his legs and when I switch on the light with that 22 mag in my right hand, he grins and it's the kind of a grin that says do you really think you can do anything to me with a mortal revolver.

It's the kind of a smile that says this is my spirit machine gun, my shaman machine gun, my skin walker machine gun, my once and for all time forever machine gun.

Back, when my old man still thought of himself as a writer, his clothes crawled with stories. I'm not sure if he ever really knew that. I never told him but I always thought that he somehow did even if it wasn't something he knew in the day time. But when he was drinking and smelling of bar whiskey and beer wash he was lousy with stories.

I could almost see them snaking out of his clothes like he was alive with them the way some people have lice coming out of their shirts. When he was drinking he could tell one story right after another without ever missing a stroke.

Timing, that's what it was. It's timing the way that the body knows and timing in stories when everything just connects.

"Ever hear the one about Long Jimmy Black and his magical mystical mother of a spirit gun?"

Once my father announced a story, the men at the bar would crowd a little closer and somebody would buy my old man a shot as part of the ritual and he'd send it down the meat hatch and begin:

"Seems as though Long Jimmy found himself wandering down old Route 66. He had no idea of how he got there, but he figured one of his drinking buddies had opened up a car door and kicked his ass out.

So, there he was, stinking drunk and stumbling down the road and suddenly, straight out of nowhere this guy appears, just as though he'd just right out of the heart of a boulder. Now, the stranger can see that Jimmy is drunker than a lord, so he decides to have a go at poor old Jimmy.

He starts out by calling him every name in the book. Jimmy pretends he doesn't hear anything and just keeps walking. The stranger finally gets bored and edges a little closer but Jimmy doesn't cop to that. He just keeps lunging along through the dirt and the gravel at the side of the road.

Then the stranger goes a little closer until he is so close to Jimmy they are almost touching. The moment Jimmy looks up at the stranger, the stranger realizes he can't escape and Jimmy lays hands on this guy and they go at it, rolling around and around in the weeds and finally the stranger reaches the conclusion that he is no match for old Long Jim and says, let me go and I'll grant you whatever you wish for.

Now, boys, this isn't one of those three wish stories. We all know they can go on forever. So, Jimmy says, who are you, the devil? The stranger says, I've walked through ten thousand years of skin, fire and water. If you hold onto me too long, I'll die and you'll die with me. If you promise to let me go, I'll either grant you the wish of all wishes or I'll give you the spirit gun.

"What is a spirit gun," Long Jim asked.

"You've never heard of a spirit gun?"

"Can't say that I have," Long Jim replied.

The spirit gun is the dream of America. Jesse James had the spirit gun for a little while. He left it on the dining room table when Bob Ford shot him.

Billy the Kid accidentally dropped the spirit gun off a ledge up on Capitan a month before Pat Garrett and a Colt 45 told him a death time story while the lightning was flashing.

John Dillinger left his spirit gun under a seat at the Biograph theater and you know what came next.

Long Jim said, "Give me one wish why i wouldn't want the wish of all wishes instead of the spirit gun."

The stranger leaned close and Long Jim saw an inch of fang coming out of his mouth. Because, he said, the spirit gun is the wish of all wishes and the dream of America. If you have that, the stranger paused and took a deep breath that was wet with longing, then; you have the key to practically everything.

"If i own the spirit gun," Long Jim said.

"Nobody ever owns the spirit gun. Some say it owns you. But, if you are careful, it will do anything you want for as long as you live."

"Anything?"

"Anything, because it is the shadow and the dream of America."

"What did it look like?" the railroad man standing next to my old man asked.

My old man finished his beer, waved the bartender over and said, *"Let's have another"* and then replied *"Long Jim let me have a look at a Thompson once. It was the prettiest thing i ever saw."*

"You saying it was a Thompson sub machine gun?" the railroad man said.

"I'm not saying anything. All i saw was a Thompson, period."

"You never saw the spirit gun, then, right, that's what you're saying?"

"I know this much. The spirit gun can be anything you want it to. Colt 38, Smith and Wesson, Winchester, Thompson. The power of the spirit gun is it gets into your dreams, moves right in and lives there, but you never really know it, you don't feel anything, but you secretly want it to be there, that's how powerful it is, it burrows in and pretty soon you don't see the spirit gun. You see what you want to."

The bartender passed the beer across to my old man and said, *"Nice story Earl. Who's paying for this round?"*

My old man hoisted the beer and said *"The spirit gun's got this one!"*

I don't know how many times I heard my old man tell the spirit gun story, maybe a hundred, maybe a thousand. At least it seemed that many to me, and he never told the same story twice. He'd say kick it around a little, add something, take something out. You control the story it doesn't control you, which is so good about the telling.

The taste of the booze and the taste of the story get all mixed in and pretty soon the story is talking to the booze and the booze is talking back. The story's gotta be 90 proof or it ain't worth a shit.

But that spirit gun story. It always felt like he was holding a little something back. Like he knew a whole lot more than he was telling.

The Images of Lethal Desire

When I was a kid there was a ratty hotel down by the railroad tracks that had a whore house in it just like the one where I lived. And, you could smell that joint a block away. It gave off an odor of old rags burning, urine, rotting garbage, soiled clothes, and shit. But, it really didn't disgust me because I had gotten used to it from where I lived.

What drew me to this fleabag hotel was the antique gun store right next to it and from what I'd been told, was managed by the owner of the hotel. This was back in the 50's when old guns were plentiful and this guy had the window of the store loaded with six guns, flintlock pistols and rifles, blunderbusses, Kentucky rifles, derringers, boot pistols. He had practically every kind of old firearm I could think of. Once, when I tried to go inside and look around, he stood at the door and said, *"No kids allowed."*

So, I'd press my nose against the window and stare. I've always liked weapons. They appeal to my dark side. I used to carry a small hunting knife tucked up my coat sleeve. And, whenever I could get my hands on one, I've carried switchblades. This was when I was a kid and regularly prowled bad neighborhoods.

But I never forgot that old gun store and the sight of all those old and exotic firearms. And, this guy had blades as well. Mostly, he carried swords, though I do recall that he also had big, evil looking bowie knives displayed against wooden boards. I especially liked the blades.

I'd press my nose to the glass, and the guy would get all pissed off and thump on the window for me to get back. Sometimes, he'd even flip me off and I was always tempted to flip him back but then if I did that I was afraid I'd be 86'd from staring at the guns so I pretended not to see him do that.

And, the one thing I wanted to do was look at those guns, because there was something about guns that had the mystery of death about them and I wanted to know more about death and my father never liked to talk about it and death of some kind was always there in the movies and on the railroad tracks where a guy had been cut in half by a switch engine and in the river where one of my friends had drowned and in the guns some of my friends and their fathers had.

If I went to this gun store and stared at those guns, maybe by just staring at them I could find out something about death. And, I could also find out something about the Civil War and the Indian wars, and maybe I could also find out something about the fake deaths in all the movies I used to go to. Because maybe the fake deaths were in some way related to the real deaths that happened every day. The big death which took you out and you never came back.

I didn't know it then but I was already studying the stuff that poetry is made of. And, I didn't want to go to the books. The books smelled of school and school smelled of work and boredom and a lot of the shit I'd been running away from. I needed something else, something that smelled of the soil, fresh air, the grass, the trees, but also smacked a little of the dangerous and guns and knives were dangerous.

Guns and knives had death inscribed secretly inside them. Guns and knives held the stories of what I thought it felt like to be alive but also what I dreamed it must have felt like to be hurt and dying.

I knew, I was absolutely sure that guns and knives carried all the stories of our secret wounds and longings and I wanted to know all about those things, I wanted to study all the ways those wounds and longings made us real and vulnerable and alive to all the kinds of death floating in the air around me.

I didn't know just how much a poet I was then. Even though I hadn't written a line of poetry and wouldn't since I and all my friends thought it was a sign of weakness, though when I was alone I used to make up stories and had some of the same lines going through them to give them more power and effect. Just like in music.

The Dark Side of America

The dark side of America in Kansas City, the dark side of America in Pittsburgh, the dark side of America in El Paso, the dark side of America in St. Louis, the dark side of America in New York City, the dark side of America in Chicago, The dark side of America in New Orleans. The dark side of America is always out there and the dark side of America is always in here.

The dark side of America smells like burnt toast, the dark side of America smells like stale wine, the dark side of America smells like vomit laced with red chile, the dark side of America smells like garlic smeared on bullet lead which is just seconds away from being fired into a man's kneecap, the dark side of America smells like cheap perfume and armpit hair, the dark side of America reeks of soap and crotch, the dark side of America tastes a little like snot, the dark side of America is a fuck finger caked with shit.

Shorty and I saw a red car come down the street and hit a little black dog. Sometimes when a car hits a dog, it will just run over the dog's body, the car going bump like it hit a branch or a pothole but this time it almost looked like the dog was trying to jump toward the car and got hit full in the chest and flew over the hood.

Sometimes I can see it in slowmo even now. At the time it made me feel a little sick but also a little excited like this was death in the raw and I didn't have to pay any money for it like at the movies where all deaths are fake.

And I can remember that dog coming down and hitting the pavement kind of like a pound of ground beef that my old man has slapped into the big iron frying pan that he rescued from the dump. The slap of the meat woke me up and then the driver pulled over to the curb, rolled down his window and said," *That your dog kid?*"

I looked over at the driver. He was ashing his cigarette out the window like nothing had happened. I replied, "*No.*"

He thought about it a couple of seconds and said, "*Okay but here's a buck anyhow to keep your mouth shut.*" He tossed it out the window and drove off.

The red car burned rubber all the way to the telephone pole at the alley. I looked over at Shorty who was touching the dog. He glanced up at me, said "*It ain't moving but it's still warm.*"

He waited a couple of seconds, and then said, *"Does it look like it's smiling to you? The fuck?"*

Rick pulled up his pants leg and showed me the bullet wound. It wasn't what I had imagined. I thought I would see a hole in his leg that would go to the bone and that there would be blood going all around the bone but it wasn't like that.

I just saw this scooped out place in the pale skin of his leg. It looked like a scar and it didn't look like a scar. I don't know exactly what it looked like but it wasn't what I expected. He touched it with his right index finger and said, I wasn't supposed to get shot.

My old man's finger just touched the trigger and the gun went off and he was down on his hands and knees trying to make the hole go shut. But it wouldn't because I don't think it wanted to. He had another shot of Beam before he called the cops and they said it was an accident.

I go to the movies now just to watch guys get shot to see if they do what I did. Some nights I swear to god I can dream with this thing. I never told him but I always thought his dreams were filled with the images of scars.

Red asked me *"How come you like guns so much?"*

He was going into a prize fighter's stance and motioning me to come at him. I backed up several steps because I knew he had a really nasty right cross, I'd seen him knock kids down in the gravel and then kick them and I'd made up my mind I wasn't going to be one of them.

"What are you, a chicken?" he said, doing the thumb on the nose thing like Cagney.

"You like guns, right, he did a couple of quick jabs at some phantom in the air and moved in low."

"Yeah" I said.

"Well, why doncha say why you like guns."

"You tell me" I said dancing away from an uppercut that was already ten feet out in front of me.

"You a wise guy?" he said, making moves like a prize fighter and Fred Astaire both at the same time. *"its death, isn't it?"* he said, still moving around.

"It's history" I said. *"Gunfighter history like Billy the Kid, Wyatt Earp, you know the Old West shit."*

"*It's death*" he said. "*Guys who say history really mean death, but death is okay, death means you are a little fucked up and that means you are human.*"

"*I'm not fucked up*" I said, even though I knew I was a little fucked up but I never told anyone that. You didn't talk that way to kids who could beat the shit out of you for just standing in the wrong place.

Then he went "*Wham, wham,, got him, knockout!*" He stopped for a moment, the fight was over. He looked at me and said, "*It's okay to be a little fucked up and you know what, you never heard it from me.*"

Jerry was just standing there and the freight was starting to crank up the speed. To the left of us was a small holding pen for cattle and beyond that a hobo woods and beyond that the river.

Jerry said, "*You ever wanna drown in the shit of that river?*"

And I yell, "You *asshole, you trying to get yourself killed??*"

"*I'm playing chicken*"

"*That freight ain't gonna turn away*"

And Jerry gives me the finger so I get up on the tracks with him like okay if he's gonna stand there then I'm gonna stand there and he shoves me almost like he's trying to get me to fight him and the train is bearing down on us now.

I can feel the tracks shaking and the heat coming off that big engine's steel and then Jerry shoves me again and that did it, something went crazy fucken haywire in my head and I grabbed him as hard as I could and pulled him away and we both went down the weedy embankment and he was screaming "**fuck!**" all the way down.

When I looked up the freight was lunging past dragging bits of scrap paper with it and some of the gravel came down on top of us and Jerry was laughing.

"*What the fuck were you thinking?*"

Jerry replied, "*My old man said I would never amount to anything and I just wanted to show him.*"

"*So you tried to take on a train. Was he watching?*" I asked.

Jerry smiled and said, "*Fuck no, he's probably getting shitfaced in some dingy bar.*"

"*Then if he wasn't watching, what good was this?*"

Jerry smiled around the dark places in his teeth, pointed to his head and said, "*He wasn't watching but he really <u>was</u> watching.*"

Cowboy liked to play Russian roulette with a Smith and Wesson 32. It was a break open pistol where the barrel would pop down and you'd load the cylinder while all those black cylinder eyes were staring at you. Once he showed me how it was done.

We were standing between two garages behind the hotel where no one could see us and he took all the bullets out of the revolver and then put just one in. I watched him do it. He held that bullet between his thumb and index finger and slid it in. Then he clicked the barrel in place and spun the cylinder and it went around a couple of times, maybe three and stopped. He looked over at me.

Cowboy had one of those square faces where the skin was drawn tight over bone and if he ever smiled I never saw it.

He said, "*You wanna play?*"

"*You go ahead*" I said. "*I'll just stand here and watch.*"

"*You like to watch shit like this, don't you? Some guys get off on watching.*"

He lifted the revolver, his hand came up quickly, faster than I expected. He put the gun barrel point first in the hair above his ear, pulled the hammer back and I braced myself for the explosion, but all I heard was a click.

"*Want me to go again?*" he asked.

I gave him a nervous smile and said, "*Fuck yeah!*"

He repeated the motion. Pistol up, barrel in the hair, click. Again, he asked. I didn't say anything. I was sure he was going to blow his brains all over the garage wall and after that I didn't know what. Before I could answer, he repeated the action one more time. Click.

Then he did a quick gunfighter spin, stuck the pistol in his belt, put his thumb up to the side of his nose and blew snot all over the garage wall.

"*You didn't have any shells in that gun*" I said.

Cowboy smiled and said, "*Maybe yes maybe no. Maybe I was just trying to fuck with your mind.*"

"*Show me the gun*" I said. He just grinned, gave me the finger, and walked away. Maybe five steps into the walk, he glanced back and said, "*Sweet dreams kid.*"

"Why do you wanna be a writer?" Roy asked, knocking some ash off his roll your own.

"*I wanna make a lot of money, leave this shit pile of a hotel and be somebody.*"

Roy shrugged and said, *"Maybe you could write a movie. But if you want me to like it, it better have a lot of shooting in it. Like a western"*

I said. *"Yeah, a western would be fine. Also, a gangster movie."*

"I just like shooting" he said. *"You ever see anyone get shot?"* I asked.

"A long time ago in Chicago" he said. *"A guy came running out of this bar, blood on his shirt, I thought he was faking it. Like he'd poured ketchup all down himself and I was gonna yell some smart ass shit at him and he fell down on the sidewalk and I thought he was just playing dead like you do when you are a kid and I went over and touched him with my shoe and he never moved and some cop walked over and hit me with his night stick and I never even did anything.*

Then he hit me again and I fell in some dog shit and I was afraid to move and he said, "get the fuck outta here kid before I run you in" and I did and while I was running I looked back and saw some guy walk over to the cop and give him some money. Roy paused, flicked some more ashes and said, *shooting in the movies sometimes clears up the head."*

"From what?" I asked.

"The dreams" he said.

"The dreams."

When my old man wasn't drinking or hustling a scheme with some local gangster he was whittling a piece of wood. I still have the jack knife he used to whittle me a wooden gun.

He carved it out of a cheap piece of wood he'd picked up while doing a fire department inspection at a lumberyard. This was just before they kicked him off the force for drinking on duty. I remember him sitting on the front step, a bottle of Jim Beam jammed down inside his jacket for quick hits while he worked.

At first I didn't know what he was carving. And, he didn't volunteer any information. He'd just sit there making little cuts in the wood, then shaving the surface smooth. His pants legs were starting to get covered with wood shavings, when I finally said, "are you making a gun?"

He blew all the little bits and scraps away from the surface, sighted down the length of the wood and said, *"You know what happened to the guy who asked Machine Gun Jack McGurn too many questions?"*

"No" I replied.

My old man paused for a couple of beats and said, *"He was staring through all the holes that Thompson made in his clothes."*

After that I went somewhere else so my old man could work and when I got back a few hours later, the gun was finished. He was still working the rough spots on the barrel when he finally just passed it over.

"It ain't much" he said. *"It's supposed to be an automatic but it's a little crooked in places and the grip has some bumps. Otherwise, it looks good. One other thing, you'll have to paint it black if you want it to look like Dillinger's gun."*

"Dillinger's gun?" I said.

"Yeah, the one he used when he escaped from Crown Point."

He took a hit of Beam, then said, *"Second thought don't paint it black. No wooden gun could ever be as good as the one Dillinger had. Still, it needs a little something extra."*

He fished a sack of Bull Durham out of his shirt pocket, took out a cigarette paper from a little book of papers, tapped some tobacco into it, sealed the paper shut with some whiskey spit, lit the end, and inhaled. Then he blew whiskey smoke all over the barrel, winked, and said, *"If that don't magic it up then goddamit nothing will."*

I called him Stick because he was always breaking sticks in half and throwing them out into traffic just to see if any drivers would slam on their brakes or slow down and when they did and it looked like someone was going to pull over, get out, and come running after him he'd take off down the alley and once he did that he could never be caught.

Once, when I asked him why he threw sticks at cars he said, I like to fuck with people's heads. Then the match he held between his teeth would go up and down like he was trying to see if by moving it around he could somehow scratch up some fire in the air.

I always wanted to ask Charles Bukowski what it felt like to be writing out of the dark side. He's writing very late at night and while he writes he notices that all the words float out of his typer and blacken the air. I always wanted to ask T. S. Eliot what it felt like to be writing out of the dark side. The shadow he walks with every day at noon begins to tell him things he puts into <u>The Waste Land</u>.

Maybe that's why he suddenly became so religious. The whole process had fucked with his head. I always wanted to ask Walt Whitman what it felt like to be writing out of the dark side. I like to pretend that he walked way back in the woods and while walking found an old rusted trade tomahawk with some old blood and hair plastered to the steel. And, because he was so far back in and there was no one around to see what he was doing, he tasted it and discovered that it didn't taste bad.

I always wanted to ask Cormac McCarthy what it felt like to be writing out of the dark side. I have this vision of him buying a human scalp from some antique dealer who specialized in the historically peculiar and while McCarthy was working on the novel he kept the scalp draped over a door knob in the room where he worked and sometimes at the odd moment he could feel some strange energy climb off it and go into the air. I always wanted to ask Ernest Hemingway how it felt to write out of the dark side.

Every time I read After The Storm I see him finding a corpse washed up on the beach at Key West and when he searches the body he comes across a jack knife which gives him the idea for the story. And, the jack knife is such good luck he carries it in Africa for all the big kills.

I always wanted to ask F. Scott Fitzgerald how it felt to write out of the dark side. I can see him one night coming out of this speakeasy drunk and he looks down, sees a human tooth, picks it up and gets the idea for a character in Gatsby called Meyer Wolfsheim.

The second my old man pulled his molar with that old pair of pliers he passed the tooth on to me, leaned over the sink as far as he could, and puked. It took him three tries to get it all out and the stuff that wouldn't wash down the drain he picked out with his fingers and threw in the toilet.

Then he went in and sat on the edge of the bed, drinking Beam, gagging, spitting blood and pus out in an old rag and then drinking more Beam.

"Finally" he said, *"I heard it pop free, didn't you?"*

"Yeah" I said. *"I could hear it across the room."*

"Son of a bitch, I think the roots are still in there. Maybe they'll word themselves out. The worst thing is the pus. It keeps trying to go down my throat."

He took another hit of Beam. Then he said, "take that goddam tooth out and throw it in the fire barrel. Be sure you put enough dry shit in with it so it'll burn up good."

I took out some old newspapers and rags and got a good fire going and I pretended to throw the tooth in. Instead, I palmed it back into my jacket pocket. For some peculiar reason I wanted to walk around with my old man's tooth in my pocket. I wanted to feel it there against my hand, I wanted to have it knock against my leg, I wanted to see if I might be able to get a story out of it, I wanted to take it out and look at it in the dark. And, I wanted it to make me feel dark, so very dark all over.

Sonny Paige sat in the dirt behind the hotel. He had a big jagged piece of concrete in front of him and he was using a claw hammer to smash something. His hammer swings went high and came down hard and each time he brought that hammer into whatever it was he was wrecking he'd say, "there, now I kill you again."

I couldn't see what he was beating into a pulp until I got close and realized he was pounding a cheap 22 revolver into pieces. The trigger guard was already bent and the snub barrel had gone crooked and nearly flat under the hammerings and Sonny looked up at me.

He had a pushed in face and eyes that went sideways whenever he talked. He said, *"This is the gun my dad used to kill hisself with and now I gonna kill it."*

Some spit came out of his mouth when he said *"kill"* like he was trying to somehow eat the word up so that nobody could ever say it again.

Then he hit the pistol one more time so hard that the gun's hammer broke off and he picked it up and stuck it in his mouth.

"It kill my dad so I gotta taste it."

When he finished I helped him pick up the pieces of the revolver and we walked over to the fire barrel where we dropped them in. He said, the fire burn it up and I shook my head yes knowing that all the fire might be able to do was scorch raw death out of the iron.

The wooden gun my old man had carved for me turned out to be my good luck charm. I liked to carry it jammed inside my coat. And, because it was small enough I'd often stuff it down inside my right trouser pocket. Just to have it there, just to feel it ride against my leg made me feel lucky.

Then one day several months later it turned up missing. When I asked my old man if he had seen my wooden gun, he said *"What wooden gun?"*

"I said the one you made for me"

He said "*I never made you any wooden gun*"

Then he added, the only kind of gun that is worth a shit in this world is a real one. Bang bang bang bang.

I never bothered him about it again.

Excerpt from the essay
Scorched Trinity: Dillinger, Billie, and Machine Gun Love

I saw a guy stick up a bank with a machine gun once. The man talking was a drifter by the name of Lucky Jack Ross. He was someone I met at the Clifton Hotel. Yeah, I saw this guy come into the bank with a machine gun. It was payday on the railroad. That's when I lived in Kansas City. The whole thing happened so fast, and, smooth. Christ, the way this guy handled himself, it almost looked like he was dancing.

But, it was his machine gun that got everyone's attention. I don't think the man said a dozen words the whole time. And, he never raised his voice. I already had my money and was about to drop it in the sack when he looked at me and said, "*You work in a factory?*" I looked straight into his eyes and said, "*No, the railroad.*" He smiled and said, "*Keep it, pal. You guys work hard for the money.*"

The bartender at Blackjack Willie's told me once his old man had been on the police force at the time of the St. Valentine's DayMassacre. He said, he was one of the first to arrive on the scene. The way he described it, it must've been a helluva sight.

They used both shotguns and machine guns. Machine gun slugs had cut this one guy in half right along with his necktie. Said, another guy was lying on his side on the cement floor and the blood coming out of his mouth looked like all of his words had poured out in a red puddle.

Excerpt from the essay
Mythic Blood, Psychic Movies, Outlaw Dreams

We live by the blood of our stories. We live by and through the blood of our stories. The blood of our stories and the myths of our dreams. My father lived off that blood for as long as he could and died wrapped in his dreams. He was my father when I loved him and my old man when I tried to distance myself from his whiskey lunatic schemes.

I will never really know just how much he made up and what was the truth. He liked to talk about my great grandfather, who probably rode with Quantrill, though his name never appears on any of those rosters.

He liked to talk about seeing Al Capone get off a train down in the Illinois Central yards and that very likely did happen. And, once or twice he talked about buying John Dillinger a beer in a Chicago speakeasy. Maybe that happened and maybe it didn't, but the way my father told it, the incident somehow became the kind of cinema I couldn't get out of my head, then or now. It just kept coming back in all of my psychic movies.

Later, when we were living in the hotel, I remember a cop coming by to see my father. The cop always carried a silver flask inside his coat. He and my father would kill the bourbon contents of it out behind the hotel. After they finished, the cop would motion me over and say, "Wanna see Dillinger's automatic?"

I'd seen it before but I never got tired of looking.

My father would take a long drag off his cigarette, flick it into the gravel and say, "*Tell me how you got it, again.*"

"*Poker game in Dodge City, Kansas*" the cop said.. "*I was out there visiting my uncle and one night we all went to this private club, got into a poker game and it was my lucky night. This retired bank guard from Mason City, Iowa, lost all his money and the only thing he had left to bet with was this automatic.*

Said he was a guard when Dillinger and his gang robbed the bank there. The guard said, "I was on duty that day. Dillinger and his boys were on their way out and Dillinger was trying to juggle a bag of money, a Thompson machine gun, and the 45 auto and the 45 just came out of his hand and slid across the floor. I heard him yell, no time, just leave it.

Once they were out the door, I picked it up. The head cashier said, you'd better turn that in to the police. I just smiled at her. I never told her it was just the kinda dream I was waiting for."

The cop let me hold it.

The 45 felt a lot heavier than a cap pistol. I looked at the cop, said, *"What did the bank guard say when you put the winning cards down on the table?"*

The cop grinned and said, "What *do you say when your dreams are all gone?"*

Before I could hand the 45 back to the cop, my father took it out of my hands and stood there awhile running his hands up and down the barrel.

"Sonofabitch" he said after a few seconds. He had sweat beads forming all over his forehead. Maybe it was the whiskey. Maybe it was the pistol. The sweat beads were starting to run down his forehead when he said, kinda *"Feels funny holding Dillinger's automatic."*

"Yeah" the cop said.

"Almost like touching the man himself."

Excerpt from the essay
The Nightmare Talking

My old man passes a pint of whiskey across to a guy called Sully and says, do you still keep a Thompson under the bed. Sully takes a hit of the whiskey, holds it in his mouth for a little while, then swallows.

"Does the machine gun ever talk back?" my old man asks.

Sully takes one more hit of the whiskey and passes it back. Then says, *"In ways you couldn't even imagine."*

Once he told me a story about seeing some guy after he'd been shot to death with a machine gun, bullet holes going across his chest, he said. The whole front of him covered in blood. Said they had the body in the police station before the undertaker came to get him. He was sprawled on an oil stain near a cruiser in the garage.

One of the cops said, *"Hey Earl, you want a souvenir?"*

The cop took his jack knife out and cut a slug out of the dead man's rib cage, wiped the blood off with a rag, and said, *"Keep it in your pocket, it'll bring you good luck."*

Excerpt from the essay
Scraping the American Dream off the Slaughterhouse Floor

I'm back on the river again with a kid who has a 22 caliber pistol and a pocket full of slugs and we're shooting glass bottles off fence posts and the glass is exploding just the way I used to love it and a dog is off somewhere across the river howling at something and an old man drinking whiskey straight out of the bottle is squatting in the grass behind us and every time one of us gets a bottle he jumps up and does a little hoedown in the weeds and then yells, "*Goddamit I wish I could shoot like that again.*"

I even remember the gun. It was a Ruger that the kid had borrowed but forgot to ask for from his old man's underwear drawer. That and a box of cartridges. His old man used to call them catridges, leaving out the one r. And the way he said the word, he put a twang in it that sounded a little like Tennessee.

We both knew what would happen when he went home. His old man would be waiting with his belt in hand at the door, but then he would be standing there anyway, so this kid, call him Sonny, decided that if he was gonna get a beating for nothing, then fuckit, let it be for something after all.

I think that's when we both became outlaws. It was outlaw to defy your father, and it was outlaw to fall in love with guns the way we did, and it was outlaw to stick that pistol inside our coats.

It was outlaw to walk down the street that way, not just walk but strut down that street packed that way and loving it and loving the feeling that sometimes in America when you don't have anything but the clothes on your back and just barely a roof over your head then it was somehow okay to fall in love with knives and guns the way we did.

It was somehow also alright to pretend you were John Wayne in "*Red River*" or Humphrey Bogart in "*High Sierra*" because you stood at the very fringe of things and everyone knew your old man was an alkie or an ex-con or a thief and it was also okay to reinvent yourself, make up a mythology about yourself partly based on outlaw stories passed down through the family and partly based on movies we'd seen.

Movies and guns, and guns and movies. It seems as though the only movies i ever loved had guns in them. And, guns were okay because they were part of the American dream. I remember being over at Sonny's house once when his old man was sitting out on the front porch with a Winchester 30-30 flopped across his lap and a bottle of Jim Beam slid under the chair.

Every once in awhile he'd fish that bottle out, take a pull, then talk about that old Winchester like it was a family member, maybe a kind of super father that he really worshipped and loved.

He used to say, "*My old man told me that he got this gun from Bob Dalton just before the gang got it in Coffeeville, Kansas.*"

Then he'd rock some, take another pull on the Beam and say, "*Yeah, I'm goddam sure that's where he got it*" and he'd smile like the rifle made him feel like a million bucks.

Then he'd say, "*I don't know how many man. If you loved your rifle you didn't mark it, no sir. You didn't put one little notch on it to show you killed a man. It just wasn't done. And, see how clean this wood is?*" he'd say stroking the stock. "*Clean, oh clean, oh clean, oh clean.*"

Then he'd drink a little more whiskey and breathe in deeply so that the phlegm in his throat rattled around like gravel against glass.

After that I'd go home and my old man would be sitting at the window with one of my gun books out. i liked to buy books about Colt and Smith and Wesson revolvers and he'd have the page open and he'd be working on the Calvert and he'd point to a picture of a six shooter and say, "*I used to have one just like that. Did you know that?*"

And I'd go "*Yeah, uh huh.*" And he'd start in about how his grandfather had twin Colt revolvers.

"*Thirty sixes*" he'd say. "*Thirty sixes. When those pistols went missing, the whole world went down. Dream was gone. i'd like to have one, just one, right now.*"

"*What would you do with it?*" I'd ask.

"*You making fun of me?*"

"*No, no, just curious is all.*"

"*Why, I'd sit and look at it, I'd just sit and look at it all day, because see I don't know if you'd understand this or not and anyway it really doesn't matter if you do because I do and that's all that counts, I'd have a part of a lost America again.*"

Maybe I'd go to a movie. "*High Noon,*" or "*3:10 to Yuma*" or "*Rio Grande,*" or it might be "*The Asphalt Jungle*" or" *The Desperate Hours*" or "*The Big Heat.*" In the winter it had to be warm and in the summer it had to be cool and the images on the screen had to move fast enough for me to catch out on them as though they were freights and the stories had to click right along to keep my mind off my father's lost America.

And the popcorn had to be swimming in butter and the girls who passed along in the flickering outlaw light had to be as juicy as the ones up on the big screen and for a little while I found another version of the American dream, but it was so elusive that by the time I got home it evaporated into the dark and aching neon air.

And, sometimes I would stand out on the street in the dark in front of our apartment in that old hotel and watch the cars go by and watch the hookers go by and watch the stars way up begin swirling around in that hard unforgiving American dark, where all the sunlit American dreams get sucked into, and I could hear my father talking to himself in that bittersweet drunken voice of his in the night, fading back and forth, eventually getting lost in that darkness as well.

Chapter 7

Outlaw Writing

"My dad and I had many discussions about his father since I never had a chance to meet him. I was born in 1967 and he had died in 1960. What I didn't know until later was that he had aspirations to be a writer, I never knew. He had an interest in writing novels; I believe it was detective fiction.

After my father passed away my brother found a rough manuscript in our dad's office that Earl had written. It was a very dense, very complex 5 page philosophical essay entitled, "Simplicity in Thought." As far as we know, that's the only manuscript my father had that belonged to his father. There is no date it was written but I can only guess late forties, maybe between 1947 and 1950." To my knowledge my Grandfather Earl never got published."

-- Theron Moore

Anita L Wynn*: What initially inspired you to become a writer?*

Todd Moore*: I wanted to be a writer for almost as long as I can remember. My father, who was a railroad man and then a fireman, was both an alcoholic and a failed writer. He was a natural born storyteller and for about fifteen years tried writing novels.*

It was during this time that he got into the habit of reading parts of his novels to me. Even after he realized the futility of what he was trying to do and gave up writing, I continued to think of him as a writer.

I mention the alcoholism because that contributed both to his failure as a writer and to circumstances which landed the family in a skid row hotel for twelve years.

This really has nothing to do with inspiration, but the experiences I had in that hotel shaped me as a poet. I didn't realize it at the time. In fact, it took a college education and another ten years before I finally began to discover who I really was and that mysterious thing called style.

Anita L. Wynn: *For those readers who are not familiar with the "Outlaw" school of poetry, how would you describe it, and the poets who follow it?*

Todd Moore: *in 1949, when my father landed the family in that skid row hotel, I became an outlaw. I became an outlaw because I became an outcast. I became an outlaw, because for the first time in my life I realized what it meant to be down and out. I was twelve going on thirty.*

I became an outlaw because all of a sudden my friends were other kids who were street thieves. I became an outlaw because I was rubbing shoulders with all kinds of derelicts. I got to know all the hookers by their first names. I learned the art of shoplifting from the best.

*The word **outlaw** was second nature to me. How I escaped jail or worse, I'll never know. But I did realize that if I wanted to escape this cycle of petty crime and poverty, I'd better get an education. However, even after I graduated from college I still had some of that outlaw in me.*

Even after I taught in the public schools for several years, that outlaw was still there. Finally, I realized that my skid row background was what I was meant to write about. So, I present myself as a kind of explanation.

From the age of twelve until 1961, I lived the down and out life in a skid row hotel. Bukowski didn't really find his voice until his mid thirties. The same thing happened to me. Bukowski and I are both known for creating highly recognizable poetic styles. And, we have both pretty much been loners.

Neil Wilgus: *How did you get interested in poetry as a way of expressing your experience? Have you written any prose fiction?*

Todd Moore: *I got interested in writing through my father. When he wasn't drinking he'd read to me from one of the novels he was working on. I thought I was the luckiest kid in the world because I had an old man who could really tell a story. Then when he hit the wall as a writer, I figured I would be the one who'd write the great American novel. Trouble was I had no clue what the great American anything was.*

Then I went away to a little Midwestern university and the English professors pretty much disabused me of any notion that I could write. Or, I should say almost disabused me of that idea. But, I held onto it for dear life. When I graduated in 1962, it took me eight years and maybe a dozen novels before I realized that novels were a losing proposition.

And, it just got down to this. Could I write a decent line of poetry? Just one decent, honest, motherfucking line. Just one. That's all I was asking for. That took another two to three years of reading and writing before I hit the surface of the mother lode.

Excerpt from the essay
Blood of the Poet

I am reading in the Clifton Café to another kid who also wants to be a poet. The joint reeks of stale beef gravy and sour vegetable stew. It's 1959. The few poems that I have I scrawled out on a long yellow legal pad. The poems are anything but legal. Even then I dreamed outlaw, I dreamed B movies and gangster apocalypse.

I have a couple of poems about hookers and a couple about railroad men and a couple about alkies. They don't work I can feel it in my blood these things you know with your skin and your longing. But, I have no idea about how a poem should look and I have no idea about how a poem should sound.

Still, that doesn't stop me because I am intoxicated with the idea of just writing a poem, just getting it down on paper because I believed then as I believe now that just the act of writing somehow sets you free and I am thinking maybe Pasternak will like this and I am thinking maybe Ginsberg will like this and I am thinking maybe Kerouac will like this and two blocks away a freight is rattling past a soot blackened building and I can feel the table that I am sitting at shake a little and a fat cockroach skitters across the floor past my foot.

I let it go because this is poetry and you shouldn't kill anything while you are reading a poem an idea that I have thrown out since then you should kill everyone while you are reading you should knock the whole audience out and blow them to pieces while you are reading and the café coffee tastes as bitter as blood as bitter as a hooker's nipple as bitter as dead man's eyes and I really don't give a shit how bad the poems are because at some primal level I know how lousy they are but they are a kind of down payment on what I am going to do and I know I am going to write something I am going to write something

That will kick the nightmare right out of the marrow.

stormy weather's

on the juke in
the clifton café
donna's sitting
across from me
& black coffee
steam is climb
ing into my face
when she sez
i can sing just
as good as that
no baby you
can't i say go
ing back to the
poem i got all
the words down
& i know the
right moves yeah
i say getting 3
quick lines no
shit i do what's
that yr writing
a poem i tell her
you & that god
dam poetry she
sez i look up
donna is trying
to write her
name in the
diner water on
the chrome
table top while
lady's closing
w/raining all
the time

The Danger Writing

I was born along a skein of dark rivers -- the Pecatonica, Yellow Creek, the Kishwaukee, the Fox, the Rock, the Fever, and the Mississippi. It was the country of blood in the water and blood on the ground. The sight of the final days of the Black Hawk War, the place where some of the members of John Murrell's Gang were lynched, the hunting grounds of the Timber Wolves and the Brown Gang. And, later, the outlaw trail for John Dillinger, and Pretty Boy Floyd.

Writing is no good unless it is informed with a sense of the dark waters. Writing is no good unless it has been baptized by the threat and the dangers of all the dark waters and the knowledge of what once was known as the dark and bloody ground.

The writing of poetry is no good unless it has been rained on and washed in the blood of the darkness of waters.

Writing poetry is no good unless some of the memory and imagination and threat and animal and fish blood have somehow gotten into it and claimed it and somehow made it a home.

Writing poetry is no good unless it is stained with its primal sense of wildness, the smell of the old, and the aboriginal rank stink of tree limbs and water.

And, when these kinds of things get into the writing the whole idea of what writing is becomes edgy and unpredictable and nightmare filled and dangerous. The danger writing is what I am talking about.

The danger writing where all of it, imagination and energy and desire and the sense of having a hunting knife close by with maybe some blood on it and the dreams and expectations of what maybe the next sentence or paragraph or line of a poem might bring because the feeling of poetry is in the writing already, the feeling of going way beyond what I've already written and the outlaw sense that it's okay to have one man kill another in a poem because the poem is more real than the newspaper which is sitting on a table beside me.

I read this story in the paper where some guy shot another in a bar down on Shawnee Street next to where I used to live and while he did that the man next door was inside his girlfriend and the sweat from their bodies was soaking the sheets and it was alright to come back out of that because the news story and the poem were talking to each other.

The dead man was telling the girl it was okay for her blood to come out because his was coming out too and their blood would be separate poetries in a universe of blood and the alphabet's hum.

And, if it all gets mixed up together that's alright because somehow it all gets worked out in the line of a poem, it gets worked out the way that a drowned man's head gets cut from a fishnet, the way that the face of a wanted poster outlaw floats in the river and a guy on shore is using a 38 special to shoot at a whiskey bottle floating in the current. Its all of that.

And, the river stinks all up and down it, the stink of rotting fish, dumped chicken bones, old tires, stove boats, and the bodies of dead men who've gone under so long ago they'll never come up and all of it, aching in the heave and dredge and sweep of the current which doesn't look like it's moving but is moving in the way a clock's hands are moving.

The danger writing lies at the heart of the river, the dark waters of all the fated rivers. The danger writing includes the poet drowning in a poem so completely that there is almost no hope of coming out of it unless it ends in a rush or the ebb and squeeze of the few final seeps of it running to shore.

The danger writing demands a drowning and a resurrection. The danger writing demands everything and shakes the poet's body in the tidal lunging of its wake.

When I was a kid I used to throw stones into the Pecatonica River right where a friend of mine drowned. It was a ritual that I loved because some of the stones I let go down into the hole where his bones sat crouched and some of the stones I skipped to the other side of the river. I could control whichever stone I wanted to.

A perfect side armed throw was the equivalent of a poem and because I could only do the poems in my head then and not on paper. Those side throws only now translated into words, the rub of stones on words and words on stones.

In those days the danger writing got into writing because there weren't any rules for the way I could get words, no classroom contamination, language was still primal, my ear filled with my father's stories, the stories of his friends, gossip, street sounds, the way somebody yelled, the sound of gunfire, the sounds of things burning in the trash, no literature, just the sounds of the river of words and the river of waters.

And, I was swimming in all of it, soaked with it, burnt up with it, alive in it, in all of the danger and the love of the danger of words of it. And, sometimes somebody would say something and I'd be knocked dead smack into the heart and center and danger of it and it would be like getting pretend killed and then coming back to life.

Nothing, I think, since then has ever felt that good or that bad or that good in that bad. Poems then or the sense of poems that i couldn't write had the feelings of something rushing past so fast and so hard, only the swiftest of rivers could match them.

Or freight trains clicking past the old battery factory or bullets fired from a kid's 22, the ping of that lead piling off the old Van Buren bridge dated 1886 and climbing into high ricochet toward the river, the trees and an awful sense of feeling lost in it all. And something inside me insisted on being that lost and that wild, like a dangerous ricochet heading right for the water.

the best place

to write in the
clifton cafe
was the last
booth on the
railroad track
side the
table top
was scratched
yellow chrome
the chair
vinyl was
cracked in
3 places the
floor was
gummy
from years
of splashed
grease but
that didn't
matter as long
as the poems
kept coming
& just as
soon as i got
one going
linda the
one eyed
waitress wd
cruise by
w/the coffee
& say you
got any dreams

Excerpt from the essay
The History of Poetry

The day after an old alkie jumped out of a third story window of the Clifton with a radiator rope around his neck, my old man called me over to the desk where he worked as night clerk, reached under the counter, slapped what was left of that old rope down on the registration book, and said, here, write something about this. Then he reached across the desk, grabbed hold of my hand, and rubbed my hand across the rope's rough length.

I can still feel the roughness of it, the way it scraped across my skin. Also, I recall the dried blood on one place where it was beginning to turn dark. He glanced around to see if anyone was watching and when he was sure we were alone, he reached inside his ragged suit coat, fished out a pint of whiskey, unscrewed the lid, took a hit, and put it back.

Once he licked the whiskey drops off his lips, he said, you can't write unless you know the feel and smell of death and you can put that into a sentence. On my way out of the lobby, I glanced back and caught a glimpse of him sniffing the rope.

It took me a long time to shake the history out of history and stick it into a poem. It took me a long time to hook history and blood together the way they belonged together in a poem. It took me a long time to understand that history and blood and poetry had always been part of that rope. It took me a long time to realize that my father knew that the history of blood is a poem, or a story for that matter.

The history of blood is a story my father could never write and that somehow he was telling me that only the message was buried under the stark reality of the ritual he had performed. That was how he operated, how he lived. He could never have told me that he had become a failure as a writer. But, he could tell me a story and let me figure it out for myself. That was his style. That was his rough genius as an oral storyteller.

I am not exactly sure what became of that rope. Maybe he burned it in the trash barrel out behind the hotel. Or, maybe he gave it to some bartender in exchange for a drink. In a way, I almost favor that as a possibility.

I do know that one of his friends on the police force gave him the dead man's jack knife, spare change, and bible. I watched him drink up the spare change. I don't know what happened to the bible, but he gave the knife to me. Just in case, he said shoving it into my hand.

In later years, I wrote a couple of poems about this incident but never really got it right. Maybe it was too close to the blood, the fire, and the nightmare of those years in the hotel.

I do remember accidentally cutting my hand with that jack knife and then later breaking the blade while trying to stick the knife in an old wooden door. I never mentioned it to my old man. Just threw the damaged knife into the river where it probably belonged anyway.

Around the same time I found an old rusted socket bayonet sticking into a wooden post at the local junkyard, pried it out of that wood, and shoved it under my coat. A wino who was standing just outside the entrance to the junkyard, walked over and said, "*I saw what you did but I won't tell.*"

He was wearing long ripped up black coat that had pockets that dangled and flapped in the wind. I looked at him and said, "I don't know what you are talking about."

"*That's okay, kid,*" he said, "*but I know you took that old bayonet. It reminds me of one I used when I was in the army. Terrible things, bayonets,*" he said, spitting a stream of tobacco juice into the gutter. "*If you ever used one on a person, you'd know what I was talking about.*"

"*Did you ever use one on anybody?*" I asked. He gave me a funny look, spit again and said, "First World War. The Ardennes. He *was trying to shoot me but his rifle jammed.*"

The wino paused, then walked away talking to himself. The last I saw of him he was down near the railroad tracks talking to a freight clicking past.

It took me a long time to come around to poetry. It took me a long time to realize that I had always been a poet. It took me a long time to realize that I had always been in love with the kinds of stories that end up in poems. It took me a long time to put history and poetry and stories and blood together.

It took me a long time to understand that poetry and stories and history and blood came out of the same primal ground as the things my father talked about.

It took me a long time to see the way it all fit together, the wrecked and falling down hotel, the stinking river, the switch engines and freight trains down in the rail yards, the lost alkies, and the blood stained rope. It took me a very long time to realize that the history of poetry has always been blood.

Fuckit, I'm an Outlaw
By Todd Moore

Some people go to church to be born again. Others hit the movies. I'm in the second category. I remember I used to cheer for the bad guys in the movies maybe more than the good ones, if i liked them well enough. If they took me out of my down and out life and gave me the juice, the action, the sweats and the life for an hour and a half. That made them good guys in my book.

Any reason, anything to get me out of that whore house hotel, and anything to get me out of town. One of the ways I got into those movies in the first place was I was a street thief, a dime store bandit. Whatever wasn't nailed down was automatically mine. All the money i made off stealing went into going to the movies because looking at Bogart and Cagney was a million times better than staring at the rummies in the hotel.

Yeah, I WAS AN OUTLAW. And I loved the action, pure and simple. Stealing made me feel good.when a lot of other shit didn't. Most of my teachers up to about my junior year in high school were convinced I was no good and not worth the trouble, and to be honest, I liked it that way. You know I figured that at least I knew who the enemy was.

In those days I had enemies all over the place. The hotel was filled with them. Mainly, drifters, low level con artists, thieves, and the occasional psychopath. They were just older, cheaper versions of me. I WAS AN OUTLAW from the age of twelve, and, I liked it.

I loved the knife I carried in my pocket. I had lots of knives but my favorites were switchblades because of the way the blade clicked when I hit the little side button. Then bang it slid right into place. I loved the look of those blades and I loved the feel and I loved the way they rode in my pocket and I loved knowing that i would fucken A use it if I had to.

That's the way you feel when you're a piece of shit white kid out on the street with nothing to lose. Because, except for the clothes on your back and the few bucks in your pocket and not a lot else, that's all you are and who you are and I AM AN OUTLAW.

After a couple of college degrees and many years of public teaching, I'm STILL AN OUTLAW. When I was a kid and an outlaw it was because I was caught in a cycle of poverty that I eventually broke out of. But, it took me awhile to discover that I was still an outlaw as an adult. Not that I ever robbed any banks or killed anyone. That wasn't it at all.

The way I became an outlaw again was to write and publish poetry in the small press. The small press is a forgotten American ghetto of the arts. The small press is all but forgotten by the mainstream publishers. There is no literary press and most mainstream editors don't want to know anything about you. In fact, as far as they're concerned, you don't even fucking exist. And, I AM AN OUTLAW.

But, that's only part of it. That's just me and my background. Some years ago after I gave a reading, a guy I didn't know came up to me and said, *"Hey, I don't know what that shit you read was, but it wasn't poetry."*

He was holding a drink and I shoved him and it went all over somebody and a couple guys who were bigger than I was stepped in and took me out to the alley to cool off. My first reaction is a visceral one. Fuck the theories. With me it's strictly physical. That's why I'm AN OUTLAW.

And, with me poetry has always been physical. It's like I can taste everything going on inside a poem.

Give me fast lines, metaphors that burn like branding irons, and velocity, along with guns, women, the sex, the booze, and the fire. Plus, it's addictive. It's my shot of Jack Daniels; it's my red hot redhead in the tight black dress.

You wanna figure out Nietzsche, fine, go ahead, just deliver me a poem as sleek as a Roger Clemons fast ball, strike over the inside corner, going so fast it ignites the air. My kind of poetry is the kind that comes from dirty street murders and the kinds of guys who take snapshots of them, like Weegee. Quick black and whites of sudden death burned indelibly into the midnight air. That's why I'm AN OUTLAW.

I remember once when i was a kid the used car dealership across the street from the hotel caught fire and the whole block from the alley to our street was lit up. There was some feeling that the hotel might go too and my father, who had been a fireman, was yelling at guys he knew who were working the hoses and the big sparks were going up into the black air and cops were screaming for us to get back but the bigger the fire became the closer everyone was pushing toward it.

For a little while I thought it wouldn't be too bad if that fucken hotel would catch fire and go up because i had nothing to lose anyway except for a broken down sofa that folded into a bed and i wanted it to burn up with all the other shit because maybe on fire it would be more beautiful than the way it looked in the half light of our shitty apartment and a few of the drunks were out in the middle of the street passing a bottle back and forth and dancing while the sparks were coming down in the street.

I wanted it to go, son of a bitch I wanted it to go. That's why I'm AN OUTLAW.

Not too long after that fire, my father was sitting at the yellow chrome kitchen table nursing a pint of Calvert and he saw me with one of Hemingway's novels; i think it was <u>The Old Man and the Sea</u>, and he jumped out of his chair beet red in the face and he grabbed that book and threw it across the room as hard as he could and it slammed off the wall and fell down behind the radiator.

"Goddamit, what're you doing with that piece of shit?" Then he sat down and put his head in his hands while I teased the book out. I said, *"What's wrong with Hemingway?"* And he just shook his head and said, *"I was always on fire to get the words down but they fucked with me. i should have burned up in a real fire a long time ago."*

Other times you're an outlaw because you can't help it. It has nothing to do with theory or religion or philosophy or the movies or great rock n roll or the best kinds of booze or the worst shit that life can dish it. It may be all of that or nothing.

And sometimes you are an outlaw simply because you get an itch for oblivion. Like that line in Chandler's <u>Red Wind</u> where jealous wives are testing their husbands' throats with butcher knives. And sometimes you are an outlaw because the dice are loaded, the cards are marked, the system is rigged and permanently fucked and you've got all you can do to pretend the poem is a fat stick of dynamite and the last line is the match.

Excerpt from the essay
The Machine Gun Blood of the Poem

I tried everything I could think of to get a wanted poster of John Dillinger off a kid called Keys Gunther but he wouldn't budge. The second he showed it to me I wanted it, and I wanted it so bad that I broke out in a sweat just thinking about it. Nights I'd go to bed trying to figure ways to get it away from him.

Maybe he'd go for a switchblade. Maybe if I upped the ante to two switchblades that might do it. Every time I went over to his house I'd make him get it out. I never got tired of looking at it. He used to say "you can look at it but you can't touch it" and all I really wanted to do was touch it, again and again.

I wanted to hold it in my hand and run my fingers across Dillinger's face for luck. Then Keys would add *"This belongs to my old man and if he knew I was showing it off like this he'd kick my ass."*

Not long after that, Keys and his old man disappeared. Just skipped town without paying the room rent. My old man said they left a beaten up cardboard suitcase behind with a lot of wastepaper inside and I asked if there was maybe a wanted poster mixed in with the junk and he said no but he did find a live 38 round that he gave me.

He was tossing it in the air with one hand and catching it with the other when he said; I wish I had the gun this belongs to.

My old man always wanted the gun and the book. For as long as I'd known him he wanted it all. Once he told me he envied Hemingway but it wasn't for his books. He was jealous of Hemingway for all the guns he owned. Especially that Thompson that Hemingway used to carry on board the *Pilar* when he went deep sea fishing.

He said he'd seen pictures of it in some big time magazine, maybe Life, and he wanted one, too. I remember my old man fingering a stiff shot of whiskey when he said, if you have a gun like that and you have the book to end all books then you've done it, you're at the top of the game.

I wanted to write a novel so bad that some nights I'd break out in a very cold sweat. I was twelve years old and I'd seen how thick my old man's novel was and I wanted one that thick and that important and that magical. I wanted a novel that would knock everyone sideways.

I wanted to write a novel that would make a million bucks and take us out of that fleabag hotel. I wanted a novel that I could sell to the movies. I wanted a novel that Humphrey Bogart might star in. I wanted a novel that would be the beginning and the end of all novels. I didn't know who Faulkner was but if I had I would've wanted to knock him on his ass.

I'd watch my old man take his novel down from a shelf. He kept the manuscript in a red folder that had strings on the sides and he'd untie the strings and lift the typewritten pages out and he'd let them spill across the table like they were cards from a lucky deck that he could shuffle and reshuffle and then he'd square the manuscript into a neat pile and sit down and study it, his cigarette half sprawling half dangling out of the corner of his mouth.

And, he'd pull a bottle of Beam across the table almost casually, along with a shot glass and while he was pouring himself a shot he'd say, this is the one, this is numero uno, the number one baby. We'll all make it big with this one. That never happened.

my old man

had his de
tective novel
sitting in
front of him
the man
uscript pages
near the
top of the
stack were
stained w/
brown drink
rings &
places where
he'd written
notes abt
where to in
sert what
you think you
cd write
something
this good he
sd taking a
long chug of
whiskey out
of a tall wa
ter glass this
is the real
shit he sd
he was
shaking &
it sounded
like he had
a fish hook
caught deep
in his throat
when he sd
i paid hard
for all these

words you
have to die
if you want
to dream

All the way to the Blood: Becoming an Outlaw Poet

I was standing on the bank of the Pecatonica River along with a kid called Jerry. We each had 22 pistols and maybe 30 slugs between us. They made funny little clicking sounds in my pocket and I liked the feel of them there and in my hand and when I fired them at the bottles Jerry threw into the river.

I wasn't that good of a shot but every once in awhile I'd get one and it would sink into the river's thick darkness and Jerry would say, *"Fucken A. Who are you now?"* and I'd reply, *"Hey, goddamit, I'm Billy the Kid,"* and then we'd go awhile and the next bottle I got, Jerry would laugh and say who are you now, and I'd say, *"John Dillinger. Dillinger all the way to the blood."*

And, I think that's how poetry got started with me. It began with a very dangerous kid's game and it took a U turn and became a very dangerous adult's game. Only it didn't occur to me then and it only quietly took over like a slow dream waiting to be born and when it finally did become a reality it just seemed so natural I didn't see what was happening until it was in my bones and in my dreams.

Sometimes during the shooting Jerry would turn to me and say, *"I wanna be a trucker when I grow up."* Then he'd cut loose at a crow in midflight and get nothing but air. And I'd say, *"I'm gonna be a writer."* And, he'd say, *"Fuckit, all you get is C's in school, how you gonna write anything."* And, I'd shoot him a finger and say, *"Shit, school don't count."*

At least, it didn't for me because it never taught me anything about Butch Cassidy, the Sundance Kid, Henry Starr, the Daltons, or John Dillinger. And, I recall once, when I was going to do a report on John Dillinger, my teacher took me aside and said, *"Why don't you choose a subject a little more suitable for the classroom? Maybe a famous president or a national hero, but certainly not John Dillinger."*

She had a very insistent look and I knew a report on Dillinger was out and suddenly I had no idea who to do a report on and finally I just said to myself fuckit and took the F. The teacher didn't understand

and showed me how the F hurt my average. My father didn't get it at all and he smelled of whiskey when he put the flat of his hand across my face, but after awhile the F began to feel good.

And when Jerry found out, he said, *"How the hell you gonna be a writer when you won't even write."* Then he laughed, punched me a good one on the shoulder and said, *"Hell, I turned in a report and still got an F. Fuckit, lets help ourselves to my old man's beer."*

It was a hot May afternoon, school was out, we were throwing knives at an old rotting door, and the beer was cold and tasted so good. And I knew even then that despite the fact I couldn't put a decent sentence down on paper, it didn't mean a goddam thing because at that moment I was already a writer and I could feel the fact of that feeling all the way to the core of my bones. I was a writer and I would always be a writer. And all the F's in the world wouldn't change it. And, anyhow, I was done listening to any teachers about writing.

The other stuff I learned because I had to, I knew if I was ever going to escape from the hotel and the hookers and the winos I better listen to somebody about a job and putting food on the table but not about writing. That was my secret place, my hideout, the hole in the wall where I kept all of my true outlaw selves.

Fifteen years later the word writer got translated into poet. But I was still an outlaw and all my heroes were outlaws and all the words I put down on paper were outlaws and it still didn't matter that my sentences were still a little jagged and didn't flow right and it didn't matter that I didn't quite understand how poetry lines got that way, sort of bent up and snapped off like sticks broken off tree limbs.

It was still fun to take a pistol out to do target practice and what I learned was I could both shoot and write a poem at the same time. I would never expect Robert Bly to do something like that. He was too busy trying to figure out Leaping Poetry. And I was just busy studying recoil and flow, recoil and flow. And the way tins cans went into the air when 22 slugs hit them. And the way glass splinters flew up into the sunlight.

And, the life and death Sundance feel of that gun in my hand. Pretending to be Lee Marvin in *"The Man who Shot Liberty Valance"* before John Wayne shot him. A gunfighter's voyeur dance that morphs into poetry. And, I could be him in a poem or somebody like him, with the stance, the swagger, and the gunman's walk.

And, it had to be there, I knew more than anything I've ever known it had to be there because it was part of the American darkness and the American dream and I wanted to enter that dream and that darkness if for no other reason than to rescue myself.

Early on, editors used to write me short notes like, you're not supposed to write poems with guns in them or violence in these poems disturbs me or we only accept poems that celebrate life.

I was beginning to learn that even in poetry, there are certain rules to follow. That there is an unwritten code of decorum and if I didn't follow it, I'd probably be considered an outcast or an outlaw. And, pretty soon I thought, fuck decorum, I'll be an outlaw anyway.

This was back in the mid seventies when I was just starting out with Dillinger and I was writing poems about newspaper homicides, barroom fights, house fires, and car wrecks. I was thinking, if Weegee could take those photographs and Goya could paint those pictures, then shit I could write these poems. Not only could I write these poems, but I realized it was somehow meant for me to write these poems. I had to write these poems.

What was happening to me in the seventies was that a secret door in me opened up, little by little and I didn't realize it or maybe I did only partly and feelings in me that had been buried ever since I lived in the Clifton Hotel began to surface again.

And, I knew that if I wanted to be any kind of poet at all I had to explore all the violence and grief and rages of my childhood. I had to drag all that red hot stuff, including my attraction to outlaws right out into the poetry.

I had to shove it in there, I had to jam it in there, I had to drag it in there, I had to kick it in there. Or, maybe that's not the way it works.

Maybe I had to let it shove me, drag me, and kick me in there. It had to be that, to the full extent of what that meant or it was going to be nothing at all, because the image of the outlaw is partly what got me through twelve years of being thought of as an outlaw while I lived at the hotel. And when you are considered an outlaw, after awhile you become an outlaw.

To borrow a line from the movie, *"The Wild Bunch"* -- *"...now, I wouldn't have it any other way."*

Chapter 8

Dancing with Knives

Knives and the Dream of Knives

I can't remember a time when I didn't have a knife. I can't remember a time when a knife didn't play some part in my life. I can't remember a time when i wasn't fascinated by blades. I can't remember a time when knives weren't important in one way or another to me.

When I was a kid I grew up poor but my father always saw to it I had a knife in my pocket or on my belt. Personally, my father loved handguns, but because my mother was scared to death of them, there were never any in the house. Still, I had plenty of friends who had guns. But, it was the knife I always went back to.

Nothing could beat a good folder unless it was a very good sheath knife, and whenever I had a knife knocking against the change in my pocket, I always felt like i had a running jump on things. It was probably just an illusion, but I needed the illusion and I needed the knife.

The reason I needed the knife was that I lived in a tough neighborhood where anything could happen and I didn't want to be caught short. On at least two occasions a knife saved my life and nearly killed me. Once, in a fight, a kid came at me with a big jack knife. When something like that happens there is no time to think, just act.

I remember turning to run a few steps, then glancing over my shoulder, ducking to the right, and grabbing the kid's arm. Somehow, I got the knife away from him and the fight was over. Then, half an hour later we were back to being friends, but the sight of that knife has stayed with me ever since. And, I remember thinking, I'll never do anything like that again, though you really never have that kind of choice.

The other time, I was the problem. I used to practice out back of the place where I lived. I'd propped up an old wooden door and was using cheap Imperial hunting knives to throw at it. I considered myself a real expert until that one time I misjudged the throw and had it bounce back and hit me. If i hadn't been wearing a big cowboy belt buckle I would have been wearing the knife in my stomach.

And, I wish i had a dollar for every time I've cut myself with a knife. The time i re member most was when I was ten, standing out behind the house on Shawnee Street in Freeport, Illinois.

My father, who was a fireman, was not far away telling a friend about the biggest fire he'd ever been in, when I accidentally closed the main blade of that folder on the little finger of my left hand. I don't recall the make of the knife anymore, but I'm sure it was a Case XX, because my father loved those blades.

Anyway, the action on this knife was both wonderful and frightening. When the blade clicked shut, it went into my little finger all the way to the bone. I remember how fast the blood shot out and I even recall catching a little pale glimpse of bone. I was almost afraid to say something to my father, but I had blood all over my hand by the time he noticed and took the knife off my finger.

My father was a natural born tough guy. He hated doctors and hospitals and what he did next was something like a defining moment for both of us. He looked at me and said, *"Nothing to worry about. Just squeeze the wound shut,"* which I did. *"Hold it like that until it stops bleeding."*

Once he was sure I was alright, he turned back to his friend. That was that. I don't think he ever mentioned it again, and, neither did I. I quickly learned my father had no time for complainers.

Later on in life when I was catching a little heat from a couple of neighborhood bullies he gave me his big folder with the nasty looking serrated back. He was using it to carry as a night watchman but when he heard about my problem he gave it to me.

I can still hear him saying, *"Don't use it unless you have to. Losing with fists is honorable but if it looks like things are going to get ugly, use this. Don't let em see the blade until the last second when it's too late to duck or back away. And, don't go for the belly unless you want to spend the rest of your life in prison. Do the leg, as close to the crotch as you can."*

I remember how he looked when he said that. He was stoic and calm but broken in the face, and in splinters everywhere else. I got lucky with those hoods. It seems as though all they really wanted to do was talk a tough game.

He let me keep the knife and I carried it around for years, even after he had passed away. Eventually it went the way of many knives I have owned. Somewhere in one of my many moves, I lost it and for that I am sorry.

In certain ways, that knife may be representative of all knives, at least, for me. They have been easily acquired and just as easily given up, dropped, or misplaced. Because of this, I see a knife much differently than I see a gun.

A knife is primal. It comes out of the dark places. It doesn't matter if you bought a knife at K-Mart, a sporting goods store, or a cutlery shop. Knives still retain that dark aura of the cave. And, it doesn't matter if you see a knife as a tool, an ornament, or something you keep in a tackle box.

Knives can be tools. But, for me, they are first and foremost weapons, and it goes all the way back to the flint knapped bone hafted pieces and comes all the way forward to the Sog.

It doesn't matter if the blade is a Gladius, a Scramasax, a Ballock dagger, a Scottish dirk, a Mediterranean dagger, a Hauswehren, a Kindjhal, a Navaja, or a Bowie knife. Each knife brings its own mythology to the history of knives. Each knife contains a multitude of its brothers' dark march toward mayhem and a dance in the blood.

Where the Outlaw Poets live

It's not so much a place as it is the dark and bloody ground of the human heart. When I was a kid my father took me down to a hobo camp along the river because he knew he could score a hit off somebody's bottle there. Besides, it was more or less out and away from civilization. Decent people wouldn't go down there, just transients off some recent freight. Most of them were my father's friends or they soon would be.

These places were always covered with scrub trees and bushes and sometimes there'd be a junked car shoved off to the side. Sometimes railroad ties were shoved down the embankment and you might see a campfire going.

When my father walked by, somebody would yell, *"Hey Earl, how's it hanging?"* Then, he'd lean close and whisper, *"Son, never come down here alone. These guys know me so it's okay."*

Sometimes I would go there alone just to see if I could, just to see if I could gut it out. I always had a knife along. Switchblade or sometimes just a big jack knife or hunting knife, like a Cattaraugus 225q and I'd wear it on my belt just so everyone knew what I was packing. The whole idea was to go there and come back, to go down to the worst parts of the river or out on the island where a lot of drifters used to hang out, do it, and make it back alive.

I never knew just what to expect but that was the juice, that was the action, just like back at the hotel. I was never sure what to expect there, either, but it was the adventure of the thing. Just lay the blood down on the pavement and see what would happen, where it'd flow.

I liked taking chances because chances were all that I owned then along with the clothes on my back, or the knife on my belt, or in my pocket, or up my sleeve. The feel of the blood pumping away in my veins that was my meat and potatoes, that was what i lived for. That was *all* that was worth living for.

My father could always sense it, though. He'd get a whiff of my clothes and say, "*You been down to that camp, haven't you?*"

I'd shake my head no and he'd say, "*Goddamit, don't lie to me, I know you been there.*"

I'd wait a couple seconds because I could see the booze was working on him and say, "*No,*" again.

"Son *of a bitch, son of a bitch, what've I told you?*" I'd let it go because if i said anything i knew I'd get it.

"*You gonna answer me goddamit.*"

"*You told me not to.*"

"*Goddam right i told you not to. Did you take anything with you?*"

"*I always carry a knife*" I said.

"*You got it on you?*"

I hauled the knife out of my pocket and he said, "*Give it to me.*"

I waited a couple of seconds and when he came toward me I handed it over.

"*I need a little protection when I come home from the bars at night.*"

That was bullshit but I didn't say anything. He knew that Jerry, the barkeep at the Circle Lounge, loved knives and was always good for a drink in exchange for a blade.

"*You got any other knives around?*"

"*Only that one.*" I lied. I had another one stashed under a loose board in the floor. It was my down and dirty knife. It had a little rust on the blade but would be good for getting out of a tight spot.

"*I'm relying on you,*" he said. He moved his face in close to mine. It was swollen with booze, a big puffy ham of a face with rage howling all the way through his veins. *"Because you know what we are."*

"What are we?" I'd say.

He'd laugh the blackest laugh I ever saw and say, *"Outlaws. Just outlaws. We're over the line to hell and gone, and don't you ever forget it. You hear me?"*

Excerpt from the essay
The Sentences are Burning

Suddenly I am twelve years old again. I'm standing in front of a bonfire with a kid who has a stick I want. I don't know why I want it, I just want it. The damned thing is crooked as hell and has all kinds of snapped off places where the nub ends are dried out and sharp and jagged. Before I can say anything this kid who knows I want that stick throws it into the bonfire and I don't even think twice about it, I just reach into the fire and grab that stick out.

While my hand is in there, I can feel the heat go all over my hand and arm and even though my whole arm is in there for only a few seconds, when I take it out with the stick intact, smoke comes rolling off me and the hair on the back of my hand and all up and down my arm has been scorched off.

I can feel places where the fire has stung my skin and I do a little dance for several seconds but the quick pain goes away and I have that stick, that goddam stick is mine because I bought it with the fire and the smoke and the wood and the sting.

I used to know this kid whose old man worked in a stone quarry. Sometimes he'd come home drunk with a couple of sticks of dynamite shoved under his coat and once when I went back to this kid's house his old man was sitting with a bottle of Jim Beam on the kitchen table, a stick of dynamite in his left hand, and a cigarette lighter in his right and he was smiling.

The kid whose name was Jerry said, he's not gonna do anything. His old man heard him say that and said, watch this, and he clicked the lighter open, started it going, and lit the dynamite.

Jerry's eyes got big when he said, you better put that out. His old man had an even wider smile while the fuse burned down toward the stick. Jerry grabbed me by the arm and dug his fingers into my skin. I swallowed hard and wanted to move but was afraid to.

When the fuse had burned to within an inch or so of the whole thing exploding, his old man cut the fuse with a butcher knife and the thing sputtered out between a plate of burnt toast and a sprawl of cold meat.

The old man said, "*I dreamt I found my hand somewhere out in the yard.*"

Jerry turned and whispered, "*He's full of shit. It's still sitting in a gunny sack back at my place.*"

Excerpt from the essay
The Dark Side of America

I was sitting with Eddie G in the Clifton Café. He had just poured a ton of sugar into his coffee. Before he took a sip he said, "*What do you think dying is like?*"

I said "*I have no idea. Why, are you dying?*"

He grinned and said, "*My old man put a knife next to my face last night for not passing the ketchup.*"

"*You gotta learn to pass the ketchup*" I said.

"*Yeah, the ketchup. But what do you think?*"

"*You stop breathing*"

"*But do you stop dreaming?*"

"*No, but all of your dreams start to smell of ripe shit.*"

He gave me the finger, then said, "*fucker, is that really true?*"

"*True as that sugar.*"

"*But, can you smell those dreams that are all turning to shit?*"

"*No*" I said. "*You can't smell anything.*"

Eddie smiled and said," *That takes a load off my mind. I'd hate to spend eternity smelling my shit.*"

Chapter 9

Harry's Bar and other Seedy Joints

Harry's Bar

Harry's Bar was just a short block from the Illinois Central Railroad tracks. It was the last room or two of an old house that faced Shawnee Street but the entrance was around the corner on Chippewa. There was an old screened in porch that held a soda pop cooler and a beer cooler.

You could just help yourself and pay inside at the bar. The bar itself was maybe big enough for six guys to stand at if they edged in close, and it was slightly curved at the end where there was room to walk behind it.

The place was big enough for five or six tables at best. I'm not sure if the joint had a juke or not but somehow I think it did. Harry or one of his part time bartenders would stand behind the bar. Harry was mostly there. I don't recall his last name. I think it was something Irish.

He always wore a brown stetson cocked just slightly back on his head. This was back in the late forties and he was well into his sixties by then. He was a short guy and had a high-legged stool he'd sit on when he wasn't busy pouring drinks. It was one of those shot and beer joints though I recall the back bar being filled with all kinds of bottles.

Harry always had a story. It was never the same one twice. That time he saw my father, he yelled, *"Hey Earl, how they hangin?"*

My father's first name was John but he hated using it, so he went by his middle name.

Whenever I went with him, Harry would say, *"I see one kid. Any more on the way?"* Harry was constantly making wisecracks. He couldn't resist giving anyone the needle.

My father's answer was, *"Jesus Christ, Harry, you outa your mind."*

"I'll get the first one," Harry said, pouring a shot that went all the way to the rim of the shot glass. *"What'll you have, kid,"* he said,

giving me an offhand glance. His offhand glances usually had a little something extra in them.

"He doesn't need anything."

"You're having one. He should too."

"You'll spoil him."

"Goddamit, Earl, have a heart. You were a kid once. Besides, it's one from the heart."

"Okay, okay, give him a coke."

Harry winked like he was in on some kind of cosmic joke that I should know about so I winked back and Harry said, *"The kid's jake with me, Earl."*

Once I settled into a chair over in the corner under a calendar with a steam engine on it, Harry brought his head close to where my father was standing and said, *"Earl, have you thought about that little favor I asked?"*

Harry never whispered even when he thought he was whispering. He was the kind of guy you could hear in the middle of a riot or a brawl.

"Not so loud for chrissake, the kid."

Harry shot me a glance, took the whiskey straight down, and said, *"Earl, if he's your kid he's jake with me."*

"We don't have to advertise this shit, now do we?"

Harry shrugged, coughed up something he spit into a yellow rag, and said, *"It ain't exactly like I'm asking you to kill somebody."*

"I know, I know." My father tapped his empty shot glass and Harry poured another. Then he gave me a look and said, *"Need any chips. How's about some chips?"*

He tossed a bag across the bar and I caught them one handed. *"Sign that kid with the Yankees, Earl. Shit, he's got all the right moves."*

"The thing is, Harry, it's not exactly legal."

"Alls it is is a handoff. I give you the package, you pass it off to somebody else. No questions asked. Earl, Earl, Earl, would I put you on the spot? Now, come on, would I? Huh, would I?"

"You've been standup for as long as I've known you."

"Okay, okay. See what I'm saying?"

My father tapped his shot glass again and Harry smiled and poured another. Then said,

"Another beer, too?"

"Sure, fuckit, why not?"

Harry had the money folded in thirds. All I could see was the top bill which looked like a twenty. He slid the small wad into my father's hand and after that I didn't see where it went. Then Harry pushed something thick and dark across the bar. I tried to get a good look but Harry had it mostly covered with a bar rag and my father fished it out, palmed it and stuffed it in his jacket pocket.

Then he turned around halfway and gave me a look like maybe he was wondering if I saw anything. I made a face like I always did when I wasn't sure what to say, and Harry said, "*You gotta smart kid, Earl. He's right on the beam. How's about one more for the road.*"

No sooner was it in the glass than my father had it down. Then he finished the beer and said, "*Let's do it.*"

I grabbed what was left of the chips and we went outside. It was just getting dark and a black wind was blowing dust all over and we walked down the street and ducked into an open field and a freight was piling by and a crow flying overhead was calling to something far off in the approaching night.

My father took a 38 special out of his pocket and held it up so I could see and it almost looked like a chunk of licorice, the kind I used to get at the local grocery on the way to school and he pulled me close and I could smell the beer and whiskey on him and he said,

"*Give me your word you haven't seen this,*" and I said, "*Sure, sure,*" and he just stood there and took a long aim at the moon.

one of my

dad's favorite
watering holes
was a place
on the west
side of town
called balles'
tavern but
whenever dad
got a little
bit liquored
he'd start
calling it
balls used
to say i
love to
drink here
at balls
& the bar
tender wd
dry his hands
on a bar
towel get
out the cut
down pool
cue & say
earl it's
xmas so be
a little kind
otherwise
yeah i know
then he'd get
his whiskey
smile going
& say but i
sure as hell
like balls

i was eating

pretzels &
drinking a
coke at
a table next
to the one
in harry's
shawnee
tap where
my father
was drinking
beer whiskey
back w/a
guy from
chicago who
smiled out
of one side
of his mouth
he had a
big fang of
a tooth that
wd come out
whenever he
sd something
& it was
really hang
ing out there
when he sd
to my father
did you know
i paint houses

Excerpt from an untitled essay
By Todd Moore

I was standing outside the Exchange Street Tap talking to a guy when Sonny walked over. I waited for him to say something and when he got even he shoved me. I thought I would let it go but then he looked back on his way past and that got me.

That smirk he had on his face just dug into me like an ice pick and when he got to the alley he turned around and came back and on his way past he shoved me again.

The kid I was talking to said *"Are you gonna let him get away with that?"* and I didn't say anything but I could feel something so fucked up and dark start to crawl up my back.

I could feel all of my skin start jumping like something way down deep inside me was beginning to let go and Sonny turned around again and started back and just before he made his third pass I pulled a blackjack out of my coat and slugged him as hard as I could.

It caught him on the left side of his face and the sound of the jack coming down on him crunched a little. Sonny screamed like a girl and while he was half falling, half lunging forward, I hit him again above the ear and some blood came out in his hair and he said *"You motherfucker!"*

I let him have it next to his left eye and he went down and by that time the bartender from the Exchange was grabbing my arm and he had my jack and my old man who had been drinking all afternoon inside came out and when he saw what happened he slapped me twice across the mouth and that hurt but long after that feeling went away that jacking I gave Sonny felt good in the dark on the way home that night.

FIN

About the Editor:

Theron Moore is the editor of the *"Saint Vitus Press & Poetry Review"* which began as a print poetry zine in 2002 that he co-edited / co-founded with his late father, Todd Moore. Vitus became a web site in 2005 (www.saintvituspress.com) operating to the present day, specializing in outlaw poetry.

Moore has had poetry published by Red Fez (web site), Poetry Motel (web site), Poesy Magazine, Tree Killer Ink (Issue #3) Criminal Class Review and of course on Saint Vitus Press & Poetry Review.

He currently lives in Albuquerque New Mexico with his wife Jeanette and has two step daughters and one step son. When he isn't writing, he's a full time computer / network technician.

CPSIA information can be obtained at www.ICGtesting.com
Printed in the USA
LVOW12s1805210713

343881LV00015B/403/P